A Place at the Table

Dilly Baker is currently Director of Development at Scargill, a retreat and conference centre in the Yorkshire Dales that seeks to be on the cutting edge of contemporary faith and spirituality.

Prior to this she was co-founder of 'The Well' Community in Milton Keynes, where she also served as Team Vicar of Stantonbury and Willen in the Diocese of Oxford. She has taught Pastoral Theology at Salisbury and Wells Theological College and is in increasing demand as a retreat leader.

Related titles from Canterbury Press

Creative Ideas for Quiet Days: Resources and Liturgies for Retreats and Days of Reflection   Sue Pickering
'a veritable feast of resource material . . . a treasury of ideas and encouragement'
   Margaret Silf
978-1-85311-742-8

Creative Ideas for Evening Prayer: For Seasons, Feasts and Special Occasions Throughout the Year   Jan Brind and Tessa Wilkinson
'as well as the seasonal topics there are "hard" topics such as mental health, prisoners, trade justice . . . and the book is to be recommended for it' *Mark Earey, Church Times*
978-1-85311-643-8

Crafts for Creative Worship: Ideas for Enriching All-Age Worship Throughout the Year   Jan Brind and Tessa Wilkinson
'It is huge fun, full of ideas, clearly . . . tried and tested . . . an encouragement to the whole community to think and pray together and to bring this as an offering of worship'
   Church Times
978-1-85311-585-1

A Place at the Table

Liturgies and Resources for
Christ-centred Hospitality

Dilly Baker

Illustrations by Coralie Mansfield

CANTERBURY
PRESS
Norwich

© Dilly Baker 2008
© Illustrations Coralie Mansfield 2008

First published in 2008 by the Canterbury Press Norwich
(a publishing imprint of Hymns Ancient & Modern Limited,
a registered charity)
13–17 Long Lane, London EC1A 9PN

www.scm-canterburypress.co.uk

Scripture quotations are from the New Revised Standard Version of
the Bible, copyright 1989 by the Division of Christian Education of
the National Council of the Churches of Christ in the USA. Used by
permission. All rights reserved.

Acknowledgement is made to copyright material:
Margery Williams, *The Velveteen Rabbit*, Avon, 1922.
Ann Lewin, 'Suitable Presents', in *Candles and Kingfishers*,
Foundery Press, 1993

British Library Cataloguing in Publication data

A catalogue record for this book is available
from the British Library.

ISBN 978-1-85311-772-5

Typeset by Regent Typesetting, London
Printed and bound by
Biddles Ltd, King's Lynn, Norfolk

Contents

Part Five: Seasonal Recipes from Scargill

Acknowledgements

Special thanks to:

Ron Ayres, lifelong friend of Scargill, whose wisdom is appreciated by so many. The chapters entitled 'The Blessing of a house' and 'Bethany' are both based on creative meditations that Ron has offered at Scargill;

Jonny Wood, friend and colleague at Scargill, whose humour keeps me going. Jonny is responsible for the chapter entitled 'Conversations with a stranger';

Coralie Mansfield, a gifted artist whose work never fails to provoke a deeper exploration of faith;

a fantastic catering team at Scargill who show us all the generous outworking of hospitality. And especially to Gavin Robbin and Norman MacDonald who offer the recipes in this book;

Joan and Ossie, who set me on the way, and of course to Flossie, Theo and Chris whose banter and love keep me alive and kicking.

Introduction

For the last ten years of my life I and my family have lived in communities. The first five were spent in an ecumenical community in Milton Keynes, where 15 of us, spanning three generations, attempted the phenomenally complex task of attempting to work out a common life. For the last five years I have lived at Scargill – a centre in the North Yorkshire Dales that is home to a Christian community from around the globe.

Both communities hold in common a deep desire to live out a ministry of Christ-centred hospitality, and both communities would, I am sure, acknowledge just how fraught with difficulties is the task of putting this seemingly straightforward ideal into practice.

This collection of resources for worship comes out of my experience of and reflection upon life lived in community; they have one thing in common – they all have something to say about the extravagant love of a God who is to be encountered in the heart of human relations, in the act of rubbing shoulders with our neighbour, in the mundane and trivial aspects of living as much as in the profound.

I have called the collection of writings *A Place at the Table* in celebration of the Christ whose reckless hospitality knew no bounds and whose table fellowship consciously brought in those who had been pushed aside, excluded from the feast of life.

Studying recently at the Ecumenical Institute at Bossey in Geneva, I was fortunate to attend a number of seminars with a group of women from around the globe looking at feminist hermeneutics. It was a salutary experience for me, for when we began to discuss the characteristics of the table around which we gather to feast, in the name of Christ, it was pointed out that we in the North always assume there will be food in abundance, yet for many of our sisters in the South that assumption can never be made. Thus *A Place at the Table* also carries a prophetic imperative – it is, if you like, a prayer, offered in the hope that we will one day live out to the full God's generous hospitality one to another and there will indeed be a place at the table, with food, for all.

Dilly Baker
August 2007

Part One

A Welcome Over the Threshold
New Year and Lent

Crossing the threshold

Prayers for the beginning of worship

Leader   Why are we gathered in this place?
All   **Because together**
       we will search for the signs of God's presence.

Leader   Why are we gathered in this place?
All   **Because together**
       we will listen for the murmurings of God's Spirit.

Leader   Why are we gathered in this place?
All   **Because together**
       we will be attuned to the pulse of God's love.

Leader   And in our togetherness
All   **May we be blessed.**

Leader   Into this space
       I offer myself;
    into this moment
       I relinquish control;
    into this silence
       I settle my soul
    and wait for the coming of God.

Leader   Here we are again, Lord,
    finding our way back to you.
    Here we sit with our half-formed thoughts,
    our unfinished sentences,
    our faltering attempts to come clean with you.

    Yet you know us through and through;
    we have nothing to prove
    and there is nothing in us that is hidden from you.

Silence is kept

Forgive us our failings –
those trivial and those that we can no longer ignore.
Yes, we know we will return tomorrow,
but grant us your grace – enough for today,
Amen

Do you see clearly?

Thoughts for a New Year

Mark 8.22–26

They came to Bethsaida. Some people brought a blind man to him and begged him to touch him. He took the blind man by the hand and led him out of the village; and when he had put saliva on his eyes and laid his hands on him, he asked him, 'Can you see anything?' And the man looked up and said, 'I can see people, but they look like trees, walking.' Then Jesus laid his hands on his eyes again; and he looked intently and his sight was restored, and he saw everything clearly. Then he sent him away to his home, saying, 'Do not even go into the village.'

I wonder whether the blind man would have bothered had he simply been left to his own devices. I wonder whether there was a determination in him for things to be different, or whether the familiarity of his world gave him a certain security that he wasn't too keen to alter. Whatever his own feelings, he had friends – friends who knew exactly what was best for him (and we all have those sorts of friends!), friends who were persistent and pushy on his behalf. Thus it was through their efforts that the man who has no name found himself centre stage in conversation with Jesus. And we're told they 'begged' Jesus to respond to him.

I can't help feeling that the friends were placing a lot of store on this encounter; it mattered to them at some indefinable level, and for Jesus to have turned away would have had implications for them. They may not have been aware of it themselves but one has the impression that this man's healing in some sense had repercussions for them; his healing was a part of their becoming whole – in some strange sense they were in it together.

Wherever a community gathers in faith around the gospel, its members are in it together. Satish Kumar in his inspirational book, *You Are, Therefore I Am* (Green Books, 2002), addresses the distortion of our humanity when we see ourselves as existing independently – both from one another and from the rest of creation. 'We rise and fall together; ultimately, we all sink or swim together. We are interbeings. . . . We cannot be by ourselves alone. This means our being is only possible because of other beings' (p. 177). As a gospel community our dependence on one another, far from being a sign of weakness, is a sign of our determination to be Christ incarnate in this place. Christ calls each of us to be a part of his healing body on earth – caring, on the lookout for one another's needs, not in a voyeuristic or judgemental way, but in a manner that allows people the space they need to experience God for themselves. After all, it's a paradox that a healthy and strong church is one that is able to show its wounds, able to be the broken body of the one it claims to follow; able to be a part of the crucified as well as the risen Christ.

And then, have you noticed the earthiness of the encounter between Christ and the blind man? There is no place here for pious religious platitudes. The meeting is characterized by the physical – the exertion of the man's friends in their determination to bring him to Jesus; the touching, the clasping of hands, the saliva on the man's eyes. It speaks of a truth that must not escape us, namely, that if we are serious about following Christ, then he is bound to take us beyond our holy huddles where we mouth his praises, beyond the joyful singing of hymns and the reciting of well-meaning words, beyond the performance of our holy rituals, into a world that is hurting and messy. Christ spent his energy with those who believed themselves to be worth very little, who had had it hard in life, who never took centre stage; he believed in life's little people – those who always got overlooked: 'Blessed are the meek, the poor, the downtrodden, the persecuted – God's kingdom belongs to them.' And most of them have never stepped over the thresholds of our churches, nor are they ever likely to. We may choose to worship God in here, but we find time and again God has eluded our grasp; he has gone ahead of us, into the pain-filled places of our neighbourhood and our world, and we are called to follow.

A third element in this story that might capture your imagination is the dialogue between Jesus and the blind man. Have you noticed how the blind man's initial encounter with Jesus involved him in responding to Jesus' question, 'Can you see anything?' The man was instantly caught up in a dialogue: he had to think for himself; the onus was on him to respond; to a degree he could determine how the meeting would progress. Have you ever noticed how many times Jesus' encounter with others involved him in asking questions? He wasn't interested in patting people on the head and confirming them in their well-held positions and theological viewpoints; he was always on the lookout to push that little bit more, to provoke, to challenge, to engage, in the hope that they might be enabled to grow up into a greater maturity of faith and love.

Sometimes the questions we bring will cause discomfort in others, sometimes the questions others raise will inflict pain on our own cherished beliefs. But a church that gives up asking the questions, slowly dies. We each need the uncomfortable grit of another's challenging perspective to produce the pearl that is the shape of our soul.

And finally what do you make of the man's reply to Jesus when he asks him, 'Do you see clearly?' I've always thought the man's response sounded a bit ungrateful –

or at least not the sort of thing you say in public. It feels a bit like the honest answer a child might give Grandma having received a gift from her that wasn't quite what she wanted – it had just missed the mark, and as the disappointment is articulated, Mum is curling up with embarrassment in the corner. After all, you'd think that the blind man would have been jumping with delight, no longer blind but able to see distinctive images in front of him. You'd think he'd be yelling for joy, grateful for the dramatic improvement to his sight. But no, there is none of that here. Instead he responds to Jesus with the cautious words that betray a whiff of disappointment, 'Well, I see people but they look like trees, walking.' And so Jesus reaches out to him again.

And we rightly demand more of God. We come to this place week by week in a spirit of expectancy, eager to taste of the kingdom's food, hungry for refreshment and nourishment. And we know we will return; we know that God will always have so much more to offer us. However much we need our resting places, our watering holes, we dare not stop too long, we dare not think we have arrived. The journey continues and our sight, like that of the blind man, can always become that much clearer, that much more focused on the Christ who inspires and motivates us.

So as we step into this New Year let us commit ourselves to being a gospel community expressed through our commitment to one another, through our willingness to get our hands dirty, through our daring to ask the questions and through our thirst for God who always, only, wants the very best for each and every one of us.

New Year resolutions for a gospel community

An affirmation of faith and commitment, inspired by Mark 8.22–26

Four New Year gospel resolutions

Leader This year we will walk in the footsteps of Christ.
All **We will not attempt to go it alone,**
        but will value interdependence and community,
        believing that through it our lives can be enriched.

Leader This year we will walk in the footsteps of Christ.
All **We will not avoid the messy places of our world,**
        not of our communities nor of our lives,
        but will get our hands dirty in the name of love.

Leader This year we will walk in the footsteps of Christ.
All **We will not seek to stifle the questions,**
        however threatening they may appear,
        but will be open to the Spirit who will be leading us,
        painstakingly, into a deeper sense of the truth.

Leader This year we will walk in the footsteps of Christ.
All **We will never assume we have arrived; rather,**
        having caught our breath and gained refreshment,
        we will be ready to take the next step,
        wherever that might lead.

The blessing of a house

The following blessing of the Scargill House was offered during a New Year retreat. With a little imagination it lends itself to be easily adapted to fit the place, occasion and people of any house and home.

The intention is to stop at each 'station' around the house, with some words and thoughts, quietness and prayer; to be led perhaps with a candle, or to leave flowers at each stopping place along the way, or both.

Music – sung or played – would add to the journey.

Through the house give glimmering light . . .
and each several chamber bless
. . . with sweet peace.

Shakespeare, *A Midsummer Night's Dream*

The entrance or the main door

Pause to consider the journeys that have been taken before arriving at this place. Think of the many and various people who have stepped over the threshold. All arrive in the hope of finding a hospitable welcome and perhaps enter with a degree of apprehension and anticipation.

May the door of this house
and the door of my heart
always be open to welcome
both friend and stranger alike.

The living room

Pause to consider good company shared.

Think of the conversations, the laughter, the listening, the thinking and the tears. Reflect on the need for a place simply to 'be yourself', to kick off your shoes, to let your hair down, to relax.

And for those who visit this place, here is the space where bags are put down, where a cup of tea is offered, where questions are answered as best they can be, where the point of unwinding can begin.

Help us to release one another of the burdens we carry.
Help us to learn the art of unpretentious hospitality
with nothing to prove,
simply being ourselves,
relaxed in your presence.

The dining room

Pause to consider the hum of the vacuum cleaner, clearing up the crumbs after a hearty meal has been shared. Listen to the clatter of knives and forks as a table is set anew. Garden flowers adorn the centre of the table, and the aroma of freshly cooked food entices the guest to sit down.

May every meal be a sacrament in our hands,
may every conversation be a sacrament on our lips,
may every arm outstretched to serve point to you, dear Christ,
our host and our guest.

The kitchen

Pause to consider how much we take our food for granted; how much we assume there will be food on our tables; how we expect variety – food that is pleasing to our taste buds and our sight.

For those whose stomachs are empty and for those who are overfed,
Christ have mercy on us;
For those who tip food into the bin, and for those who scour the bin for food,
  Christ have mercy on us;
For those who cannot choose from the menu and for those who have no choice
  to make,
Christ have mercy on us.

The bedrooms

Pause to consider the rhythm of life; the need for our bodies to stop and be still. As night falls reflect upon the creativity of darkness and look upwards at the night sky. The crisply folded sheets and the spring of the mattress, the rug at the foot of the bed – all enfolding, cuddling, embracing, to offer comfort, as a child instinctively feels at its mother's breast.

For those who fear the sun going down, we pray;
for those who sit through the watches of the night, we pray;
for those who toss and turn, who yearn for the light, we pray,
for ourselves, that God may grant us peace at the last
and a final resting place in him, we pray.

The bathroom

Pause to consider the place of water in our lives: water that cleanses, refreshes and revitalizes, water that we can splash in, soak in, play and relax in, water that through our baptism speaks to us of the unquenchable love of God, freely flowing through our lives.

The bathroom, where I stare hard at my image reflected in the mirror, with only me to comment upon myself.

We hold in our hearts the many who will walk miles today in search of water,
and the many who will die today from water-borne diseases.
We hold in our hearts those who cannot flush away the pain of their lives
and those who cannot cleanse themselves of their past.
We stare into the mirror and see you dear Christ, reflected back to us,
and for this we give you thanks.

The library/study

Pause to consider the many people who have influenced your life. Celebrate the creativity of artists, poets, philosophers, novelists. Give thanks for those who have inspired your journey; those who have helped you to formulate your questions and wrestle with life.

A blessing on those who feed our minds,
a blessing on those who keep us searching,
a blessing on those who challenge our thinking,
a blessing on those who delight in our discoveries.

The office

Notes scribbled, lists of tasks half completed, quotations to improve the mind, ageing photos stuck up randomly, drawing attention away from the present; books to retreat into and provide inspiration; a telephone that interrupts the flow of thought; the persistent intrusion of email demanding an immediate response.

For those whose work is never completed and for those without any, we pray.
For those who love what they do and for those who hate it, we pray.

For those whose work gives them an identity of which they are proud
and for those whose work devalues all they might otherwise be, we pray.

The playroom

Pause to consider your own childhood. Focus on a toy that you see in this room.
Why have you picked it out? What does it say to you?

Jesus said,
'Whoever does not receive the kingdom of God as a little child will never enter it.'
And he took them up in his arms, laid his hands on them, and blessed them.

Mark 10.14–16

The chapel

I was glad when they said to me,
'Let us go to the House of the Lord!'

Psalm 122.1

Pause to consider all who have dared to pray to God in this place. For those who
have knelt in faith, and for those less convinced; for those who have entered this
place with determination and for those who've come with faltering steps.

May our work and our worship be one.
May our prayer and our action be one.
May our confession and our lifestyle be one.
May our breaking of the bread and the feeding of the world, be one.

The spare room

Consider that place where everything gets dumped; the chaotic room on which you
close the door – out of sight, out of mind. Or consider that space, set apart, just for
you – the place you retreat to – seemingly insignificant, meaningless to others, but
special for you – maybe not this spare room but the attic, the garden shed, a cellar.

God, grant me the courage to clear away the clutter of my life.
And then, free of all that weighs me down,
may I find my true centre in coming home to you.

The garden

Consider the setting of this house; the landscape that surrounds it. Ponder the varying seasons to which the house bears witness. Eye the house from all directions –

see the variety of paths that converge on it and the drystone walls that pattern the land. Sit amid the garden, safe within its walls, and listen to the birdsong, the continual song of praise.

Bless to us the marvel of creation, the wonder of life,
that we may hold all created things in reverence:
birds and animals, seeds and plants,
trees and flowers.
Bless to us the rhythm of our days;
bless our coming in and our going out.

Welcoming the New Year

Rituals appropriate for all ages and faiths

As we moved into 2006 a group of 55 people came together at Scargill, from different countries, religions and cultures. The vast majority of them were seeking asylum in Britain. On New Year's Eve, we gathered together, parents and children alike, to look back and to look forward. On New Year's Day we met together again and shared something of our hopes, fears and dreams.

The following two rituals provided the context for this sharing. With a little imagination both can easily be adapted to suit any gathered group, especially where children are present.

New Year's Eve

The setting: People are seated in a circle. A table (preferably round) forms a part of the circle and is the focal point, alight with candles. A box of nightlights and tapers are next to the table.

The leader offers words of welcome and thoughts focusing on the ending of a year – the time when we look back and recall the journeys that we have taken and how far we've come; a time to look forward and consider what might lie ahead for us in the coming year.

An explanation is given of the game 'Pass the Parcel'.

The music begins and the parcel is passed around the circle. Between each wrapper there lies a card, three in all. The recipient of the parcel reads out the words written on the card and everyone takes time to reflect upon it. People are then invited to come forward and light a candle, speaking their response to the question on the card. Others may prefer simply to light a candle and offer their thoughts in silence.

The three cards in the parcel read as follows:

Has there been someone you've encountered over the past year, who has brought a smile to your face and helped you along life's journey? Give thanks for them.

Which is the country and who are the people you want to hold in prayer as the globe spins around and you step into a new year?

Can you name one hope or dream that you have for this next year – either for yourself, for someone you love or a situation you care about?

When all have had the opportunity to light candles and offer thoughts/prayers, a song is played, allowing people time to consider the prayers of others and gather their own thoughts together.

The leader then concludes the time together with the following blessing:

> As others have been a source of blessing to us,
> So may we be a blessing to others;
> As we have shouldered something of the pain of the world
> So may we discover those who can lift the burdens from us.
> As others have left the imprint of their lives upon our souls,
> So may our lives touch others for the better;
> And in all of this,
> May we discover peace.

New Year's Day

The setting: The gathered group are seated in a circle with a pile of shoes of varying styles and sizes as the focal point in the centre of the circle.

The leader welcomes everyone and introduces the time together by talking about her/his favourite pair of shoes. Others are encouraged to share similar thoughts (some people may have been invited beforehand to wear their favourite shoes and to then draw attention to them as they speak).

The leader then focuses on three/four different pairs of footwear (pulled out from the central pile). The following examples might be offered:

> 'These are my wellies . . . I like sloshing around in the mud and the rain in them . . . I can be messy in them . . . they give me a certain amount of protection . . .

The leader invites people to hold in their hearts those who come to mind; those who are likely to need protection this coming year – those who will be vulnerable to exploitation and abuse.

> These are my 'everyday' shoes. I love them . . . I've had them mended three times and can't bear to throw them out . . . I think they express something of me . . .

The leader invites people to hold in their hearts those who come to mind; those who will be searching for some security this coming year, for a landmark to orientate them; for a familiar hand to steady and guide them.

> These are my walking boots . . . I've walked miles in them . . . Over steep hills and by fast-flowing streams . . . I never clean them but they always do the job . . .

The leader invites people to hold in their hearts those who come to mind; those who are likely to be making costly journeys this coming year, in body or in spirit, those who will have to leave something/someone precious behind.

> These are my slippers . . . I'm relaxed in them, at ease . . . they're always just 'there' by the door when I get home . . .

The leader invites people to hold in their hearts those who come to mind; those displaced people who will be searching for home, those seeking somewhere to kick off their shoes and be relaxed, those who will be seeking companionship and hospitality.

As music is played people are invited to take off their shoes (or if they prefer, to draw around their shoes and cut out the print) and place them along the floor to form the pattern of a symbolic journey.

At the end the leader concludes with the words:

> Step into this New Year!
> Travel in hope, faith and love
> and may the passion and goodwill of your God
> accompany you in every step of your journey,
> **Amen**

The gifts we bring

A retreat for Epiphany

Aim: Using the symbolism of the gifts the wise men brought to the Christ child, we explore our own journeys toward God.

Gold: The potential within each of us

Focal point   A selection of all things gold, for example jewellery, candles, baubles.

Biblical text   Romans 8.19–21 or Matthew 17.1–8

The facilitator offers thoughts which might include reading one or more of the following:

> The glory of God is a human being fully alive.
>
> Irenaeus, second-century theologian

> Our deepest fear is not that we're inadequate. Our deepest fear is that we're powerful beyond measure. It is our light, not our darkness that most frightens us. We ask ourselves, 'Who am I to be brilliant, gorgeous, talented and fabulous?', actually, who are you not to be? You are a child of God: your playing small doesn't serve the world. There is nothing enlightening about shrinking so that other people won't feel insecure around you. We were born to make manifest the glory of God within us. It is not just in some of us, it is in everyone. And as we let our own light shine we unconsciously give other people permission to do the same. As we are liberated from our own fear, our presence automatically liberates others.
>
> Marianne Williamson, *A Return to Love*, HarperCollins, 1992

> If you allow your nature to come alive, then everything will come into rhythm. If you live the life you love, you will receive shelter and blessings. Sometimes the

17

great famine of blessing in and around us derives from the fact that we are not living the life we love, rather we are living the life that is expected of us. We have fallen out of rhythm with the secret signature and light of our own nature.

John O'Donohue, *Anam Cara*, Bantam Books, 1997

One day, a few days after the liberation, I walked through the country past flowering meadows, for miles and miles, toward the market town near the camp ... There was no one to be seen for miles around; there was nothing but the wide earth and sky and the larks' jubilation and the freedom of space. I stopped, looked around, and up to the sky – and then I went down on my knees ... I know that on that day, in that hour, my new life started. Step for step I progressed, until I again became a human being.

Viktor E. Frankl, *Man's Search for Meaning*, Hodder, 1962

Questions to explore the above (facilitated by the leader):

- Where have you settled for partly living? Where do you need to come alive to God and to the world around you?
- If spirituality is that 'primal scream' that we make as we enter this world, are you still 'screaming' or has God's shout become muted within you?

Myrrh: God's healing of our wounds

Focal point   A selection of oils in bottles and containers of different sizes and shapes.

Biblical text   John 19.38–42

After these things, Joseph of Arimathea, who was a disciple of Jesus, though a secret one because of his fear of the Jews, asked Pilate to let him take away the body of Jesus. Pilate gave him permission; so he came and removed his body. Nicodemus, who had at first come to Jesus by night, also came, bringing a mixture of myrrh and aloes, weighing about a hundred pounds. They took the body of Jesus and wrapped it with the spices in linen cloths, according to the burial custom of the Jews. Now there was a garden in the place where he was crucified, and in the garden there was a new tomb in which no one had ever been laid. And so, because it was the Jewish day of Preparation, and the tomb was nearby, they laid Jesus there.

The facilitator offers thoughts which might include reading one or more of the following:

An extract from a contemporary version of the Lord's Prayer:

> With the bread we need for today,
> feed us.
> In the hurts we absorb from one another,
> forgive us.
> In times of temptation and test,
> strengthen us.
> From trials too great to endure,
> spare us.
> From the grip of all that is evil,
> free us.
>
> Jim Cotter, 'Prayer at Night', 1983, *Prayer at Night's Approaching*,
> Cairns Publications, from an unfolding of the Lord's Prayer, 2001

An extract from the children's book, *The Velveteen Rabbit*. The conversation is between two toys in the nursery:

> 'What is REAL?' asked the Rabbit one day, when they were lying side by side near the nursery fender, before Nana came to tidy the room. 'Does it mean having things that buzz inside you and a stick-out handle?'
> 'Real isn't how you are made,' said the Skin Horse. 'It's a thing that happens to you. When a child loves you for a long, long time, not just to play with, but REALLY loves you, then you become Real.'
> 'Does it hurt?' asked the Rabbit.
> 'Sometimes,' said the Skin Horse, for he was always truthful. 'When you are Real you don't mind being hurt.'
> 'Does it happen all at once, like being wound up,' he asked, 'or bit by bit?'
> 'It doesn't happen all at once,' said the Skin Horse. 'You become. It takes a long time. That's why it doesn't often happen to people who break easily, or have sharp edges, or who have to be carefully kept. Generally, by the time you are Real, most of your hair has been loved off, and your eyes drop out and you get loose in the joints and very shabby. But these things don't matter at all, because once you are Real you can't be ugly, except to people who don't understand.'
>
> Margery Williams, *The Velveteen Rabbit*, Avon, 1922

A meditation to explore the above (led by the leader)

With eyes closed and seated in a comfortable position, invite participants to focus on their breathing, to be aware of how their body draws breath; invite them to 'breathe in the love of God'. Repeat this phrase several times. Then guide the participants in the following way:

Focus on your ears, your ability to hear. Think of the sounds that delight you most and the sounds from which you instinctively recoil.
Pause
Consider the sound of birdsong in the Spring, the sound of the babbling brook or the waves crashing over the sand. Think of the haunting sound of a child screaming, the delightful sound of laughter among friends, the sound of machine-gun fire.

Breathe in the love of God.

Focus on your eyes, your ability to see. Consider the gift of gazing on beauty and consider your ability to be moved to tears.
Pause
Consider the sights from which you avert your gaze: by the press of a button, by the folding of the newspaper, by a reluctance or a resistance to understand.

Breathe in the love of God.

Focus on your mouth, your ability to speak. Think of the thousands of words that pass your lips each day – words that heal and words that harm.
Pause
Think of words spoken in sincerity and think too of the gulf between what you say and what you truly believe; consider the intensity of silence.

Breathe in the love of God.

Focus on your hands, your ability to feel. Stretch out your hands, clench your fist, open your hand, relax your hand.
Pause
Think of your hand stretched out to welcome and embrace, think of the hand that is raised in defence, in warning; think of the fist that is clenched and threatening. Think of your hand that can touch and stroke, soothe and warm.

Breathe in the love of God.

Focus on your feet; place them firmly on the ground. Think of the places your feet have taken you and the journey you have taken to be here today.
Pause
Feet can be ugly – kicking, trampling down, destroying. Consider the feet that are blistered and swollen from trudging too many miles, feet that have run in fear.

Breathe in the love of God.

Focus on your heartbeat. Place your hand against your heart and feel your heart beating. This is you; you have been fearfully and wonderfully made; God's eyes saw your unformed being long before any days had been granted to you.
Pause
Go deep within yourself, relax, let your heart and your mind unwind; let your thoughts subside, let the pool become still. God loves you. You are. God is.

Breathe in the love of God.

Frankincense: Communion with God

Focal point   Burning incense grains and sticks.

Biblical text   Psalm 141.2

> Let my prayer be counted as incense before you,
>   and the lifting up of my hands as an evening sacrifice.

The facilitator offers thoughts which might include reading one or more of the following:

> God, you have made us for yourself and our hearts are restless till they find their rest in you.
>
> Saint Augustine

On experiencing the all-embracing, joyful love of God, Maya Angelou has this to say:

> That knowledge humbles me, melts my bones, and makes my teeth rock loosely in their gums. And it also liberates me. I am a big bird winging over high mountains, down into serene valleys. I am ripples of waves on silver seas. I'm a spring leaf trembling in anticipation.
>
> Maya Angelou, poet, author, playwright and civil-rights activist

Nothing is more practical than finding God, that is, falling in love in a quite absolute, final way. What you are in love with, what seizes your imagination will affect everything. It will decide what will get you out of bed in the morning, how you will spend your weekends, what you read, whom you know, what breaks your heart, and what amazes you with joy and gratitude. Fall in love, stay in love and it will decide everything.

Pedro Arrupe SJ, Jesuit priest (1907–91)

A creative arts exercise to explore the above (led by the leader)

You will need

- Paints, crayons or chalks of a wide variety of colours
- A large sheet of paper for each participant

The facilitator invites participants to draw a circle in the centre of the sheet of paper. Then, without consulting one another, the participants are invited to think back over their lives and select colours that represent different aspects of their lives. The space outside of the circle is to be coloured in its entirety with the chosen colours. Once this has been completed, participants are invited to shade the central circle by selecting a colour or colours that best represents God to them. Once completed, the facilitator invites the participants to reflect in silence by asking the following questions:

- Where is God's presence evident in your life experiences?
- Is God seemingly absent from significant times of life?
- Is God's presence equated more with positive life experiences or encountered more in the painful side of life?
- Does anything surprise you?
- If you were to repeat the exercise would you choose to colour God differently? If so, why?

Closing liturgy

For this the facilitator will create a centrepiece that brings together all three focal points. In addition, s/he will have prepared a selection of cuttings, from national and local newspapers, that depict people and situations where life is not reaching its potential; where human life is held as cheap or stunted in its growth. These are placed around the gold element of the centrepiece.

The liturgy begins with some appropriate music, played for approximately three minutes. This is then faded out before the poem is read.

Poem 'Suitable Presents'

If it's the thought that counts,
What were they thinking of
To give him these, gold
Frankincense and myrrh?
Extraordinary gifts to give a child.

When Mary pondered, later, on these things,
I wonder if she thought that
These are given to all –
Gold our potential: gifts that make us
Royal, each in our own domain;
Incense: our aspirations, prayers
And dreams, calling us on;
Myrrh: soothing healing for our pain.
Not gifts for children,
But, like him, we'll grow.

Ann Lewin, 'Suitable Presents', in *Candles and Kingfishers*, Foundery Press, 1993

Participants are invited to focus upon the gold centrepiece surrounded by the newspaper cuttings and to offer prayers that acknowledge the gulf between our potential, as people created in God's beauty and image, and the tragic reality of some people's lives.

Each prayer may end with the following words:

. . . So may all bask in the radiance of God's transforming light.

Chant An appropriate chant may be found from the worship of the Taizé Community. See *Songs from Taizé*, Ateliers et Presses de Taizé, published annually.

Participants are then invited to share as much or as little of the third exercise (representation of their lives with colours) as they choose and in particular to respond to the question, 'Where is, or who is, God for you at this moment in your life?' At the end of each person's contribution they are invited to place a few grains of incense in the burner. Silence is kept.

Chant An appropriate chant may be found from the worship of the Taizé Community. See *Songs from Taizé*, Ateliers et Presses de Taizé, published annually.

A bottle of massage oil is passed around the group; each person makes the sign of the cross both on the forehead and on the palm of the hand, of the person next to them. As they do so they speak the following blessing:

> Gold, frankincense, myrrh –
> gifts for the Christ child
> and gifts for you.
> May they be a blessing on your journey.

Appropriate music is then played and faded out as the participants begin to leave.

To the earth you will return

A retreat to mark Ash Wednesday

Aim: to explore how our dying affects our living.

Participants are welcomed and an explanation is given as to how the retreat will run.

Centring exercise Music is played while participants are led in a centring exercise. This might include the conscious letting go of concerns that need to be laid aside in order to engage with the day.

Introductory talk

Read Matthew 16.21–23

From that time on, Jesus began to show his disciples that he must go to Jerusalem and undergo great suffering at the hands of the elders and chief priests and scribes, and be killed, and on the third day be raised. And Peter took him aside and began to rebuke him, saying, 'God forbid it, Lord! This must never happen to you.' But he turned and said to Peter, 'Get behind me, Satan! You are a stumbling-block to me; for you are setting your mind not on divine things but on human things.'

Comment on the exchange between Peter and Jesus where we see the tension that is part of our human existence – namely the knowledge that we will meet our death, that it will come to each of us in our own time and our need to distance ourselves from it – even to deny its reality: 'God forbid it, Lord! This must never happen to you' (16.22b).

Note that the denial of death is a part of our culture. Comment on advertising strategies that are aimed to keep age and decay at bay; a medical profession that tends to see death as the ultimate failure; the sending of birthday cards that make light of someone's ageing years.

Contrast the Stoic philosophy: 'Contemplate death if you would learn how to live.'

Consider examples of how bereavement or terminal illness has led people away from trivial preoccupations and provided life instead with depth, poignancy and a different perspective.

Think of the character Scrooge in Dickens' *A Christmas Carol*. Here Dickens employs a powerful form of existential shock therapy: Scrooge was permitted via the ghost of Christmas 'Yet to Come' to observe his own death. Having watched his family dismiss his death lightly, he witnesses his own funeral and kneels in the churchyard examining the letters of his name inscribed on his tombstone. It is at this point that his moment of personal transformation begins.

Is it because we die that our life is precious? Death is what brings meaning to our lives. Our mortality gives value to our actions and relationships. At one level, the advertising world understands this well: 'Hurry, hurry, the greatest sale ever! Must end tomorrow!' And we hurry like sheep not wanting to miss out on something important. After all, it must be significant for it ends tomorrow!

Consider Carl Jung and his thinking concerning life stages. Jung identified significant stages in a person's development that have to be successfully negotiated. Living fully in the present and accepting all it has to offer, Jung considered essential for mental health and wellbeing.

There is a short story from India that speaks of a man who had to spend the night in a dark, damp cell. He was terrified to move a muscle; he hardly dared breathe, believing that he inhabited the cell with a most vicious snake that was coiled in the opposite corner of the room. As the dawn rose and light crept in to his cell, the sweat on his forehead began to recede and he mouthed to himself, 'God, aren't I lucky to have come through that.' As his eyes became accustomed to the light, he dared to confront the snake full on, only to realize there was no snake – simply a length of very thick rope wound around itself.

Perhaps we rob ourselves of life when we allow the harmless old ropes to turn into monsters that have the potential to constrict our living and keep us impoverished in our hearts. 'Be not afraid,' says Christ. Our lives are a gift. Christ invites us to enter into the fullness of life, letting go of our fear of death that has the potential to inhibit our every move. He invites us to step into the light where the shadows and the monsters of our making no longer hold power over us.

Silent reflection

Sharing in pairs

Possible exercises to explore the theme

- Reflect upon the goals that you had when you were young. What are your goals now? Meditate upon this.
- Take a blank sheet of paper. Draw a straight line. One end of the line represents your birth; the other end your death. Mark a cross to represent where you think you are on it now. Meditate upon this.
- Write your own psalm in the light of your mortality.
- Can you identify the snake that is coiled in the corner of the room? To what extent does it inhibit your life?
- Write your 'real' obituary and your ideal one. Reflect on them both. Where are the gaps between them? How do you feel about this?

Closing liturgy

Opening responses

Leader   God of all life, there is a season for everything;
there is a time for dying and a time for rising.
Grant us courage to enter into your transformation process.

All   **I have come that you may have life in all its fullness.**

Leader   God of all life, there is a season for everything;
there is a time for surrendering and a time for reaching out.
Grant us sensitivity to discern the risks we must take.

All   **I have come that you may have life in all its fullness.**

Leader   God of all life, there is a season for everything;
there is a time for gathering in and a time for creative possibilities.
Give us wisdom to understand the seasons of our lives.

All   **I have come that you may have life in all its fullness.**

Leader   God of all life, there is a season for everything;
there is a time for clarity in certainty and a time for mystery in faith.
Grant us attentiveness to sense the heartbeat of our lives.

All   **I have come that you may have life in all its fullness.**

Leader   God of all life, there is a season for everything;
there is death in the midst of life and life in the midst of death.
For all this, we are grateful.

All   **I have come that you may have life in all its fullness.**

Sharing of thoughts and prayers from the day

A bowl of ash is passed around and each person marks the forehead of his or her neighbour with the sign of the cross, while saying the following words:

'Remember that you are dust and to dust you will return. Enter now into the fullness of life.'

Closing litany

Leader   From the rising of the sun to its setting
All   **My life is safe in you my God**

Leader   From the waxing of the moon to its waning
All   **My life is safe in you my God**

Leader   From eternity to eternity
All   **My life is safe in you my God**

A foot in both camps

Thoughts for the first Sunday in Lent

Luke 4.1–13

Jesus, full of the Holy Spirit, returned from the Jordan and was led by the Spirit in the wilderness, where for forty days he was tempted by the devil. He ate nothing at all during those days, and when they were over, he was famished. The devil said to him, 'If you are the Son of God, command this stone to become a loaf of bread.' Jesus answered him, 'It is written, "One does not live by bread alone."'

Then the devil led him up and showed him in an instant all the kingdoms of the world. And the devil said to him, 'To you I will give their glory and all this authority; for it has been given over to me, and I give it to anyone I please. If you, then, will worship me, it will all be yours.' Jesus answered him, 'It is written,

"Worship the Lord your God,
    and serve only him."'

Then the devil took him to Jerusalem, and placed him on the pinnacle of the temple, saying to him, 'If you are the Son of God, throw yourself down from here, for it is written,

"He will command his angels concerning you,
    to protect you",

and

"On their hands they will bear you up,
    so that you will not dash your foot against a stone."'

Jesus answered him, 'It is said, "Do not put the Lord your God to the test."'

When the devil had finished every test, he departed from him until an opportune time.

You could be forgiven for thinking that at times our Gospel writers get a little confused, or that the Church has not quite got a handle on its interpretation of the story of Jesus. Consider, for example, that only a week ago the lectionary included that magnificent account of what is called 'The Transfiguration', where Jesus in a blaze of light stood on the mountain top with three of his closest disciples, amid a brightness that would not be diminished; yet suddenly the rug has been pulled from under our feet and here we meet him alone in a dry and arid place, struggling with the hostility of his environment. What has gone wrong? One moment we are witnessing Jesus' identity being affirmed, hearing with clarity the voice of God coming to him through the brilliance of the light; the next we find ourselves onlookers at a desolate scene, where no words of affirmation or reassurance are overheard, where no sky is ablaze with the glory of God. We have a right to feel confused.

On the first Sunday in Lent, we stand with Jesus amid a harsh and bleak land-scape – that of the desert, where Jesus, having survived in it alone for 40 days, finds himself in the midst of bitter inner struggles, wrestling with all that he believed himself to be about. First he is tempted to practise magic: 'Command these stones to become loaves of bread,' says the voice of temptation. Next he is urged to call on God for special protection: 'Throw yourself down from the temple and look to God to save you'; and then he is tempted to take control of all the kingdoms of the world and prove himself a superhero: 'All of these could be yours if you will only fall down and worship Satan.' All along, the devilish thoughts taunt him, suggesting to him that he deserved better than God was giving him: 'Why should a Son of God be famished? Why should a Son of God so much as stub his toe or be subject to Caesar when Caesar should be subject to him?'

Certainly the story stands in stark contrast to the glory of last week's Gospel.

And yet, perhaps the Gospel writer knew what he was doing. For do we not need both? Is St Luke asking us to take seriously both the desert and the mountain, both the cross and the resurrection, both the presence of the most excruciating evil and the possibility of a world aglow in the warmth and radiance of love? The Christian life is a paradox and to acknowledge the one without the other might indeed be a betrayal of the Gospel.

Perhaps the personification of evil in the form of a devil that we read about in today's Gospel may not be a helpful image for us who inhabit a very different cultural context and world view from those early Christians; but we should not be tempted to throw out the baby with the bath water. After all, we cannot deny that the most appalling evil exists – in the ovens of Auschwitz, in reckless drunken drivers, in hostage takers – they are all grim reminders of the dark, dark side of the human spirit. And then of course there's not only the diabolical evil that makes the news headlines, but there is also the petty evil that lurks in our hearts – the jealousies, the lack of forgiveness, the retaliation, the fear of the other, the insecurities that keep us closed in on ourselves and distant from one another. The desert asks us to confront the reality of all of this – to face up to the part we play in the sin of the world. The desert calls us to stand, for a time at least, with Christ, acknow-ledging some of the conflicts and clashes and devilish things that lurk for us – some clear-cut for all to see, some simmering beneath the surface, causing us anxiety or fear; perhaps conflict in relationships, conflict about our own self-worth or ability, perhaps conflict in the way we organize our lives; and some of us bear in pain the deep-down conflicts of the soul, which we rarely begin to uncover.

The desert must be taken seriously.

When Jesus returned down the mountain – his face no longer visibly shining – he returned to the plains, to the raw reality of people's lives, and joined them in all the messiness of their all too human living. But the experience of the mountain top shaped him: he never let go of his belief in transfiguration – his life was a witness to it – and he knew that a breakthrough of God's glory was always a possibility, always on the cards. So he pushed, he challenged, he coaxed, he sympathized, he forgave, he wept, he hugged, all so that others might be enabled to step into the transfiguring light of God's love.

We must never lose sight of the mountain top.

As Christian people we are called to live lives that believe in the possibility of transformation. We are asked to dream into being a God-shaped world that never lets go of the possibility of transfiguration – in the people we meet, in the places we go and in the very depths of our souls. We are asked to live in the belief that God's glory is forever straining against the skin of the world and breaking out all over the universe, if only we are alive to the possibility.

The Christian life is a sham without the desert. We must face up to the failings, temptations and evil that abound in our world and in our hearts. But the Christian life is impossible without the mountain top. We need to go there; we need to breathe the air; we need to catch a glimpse of God's glory so that we have the inspiration and the impetus to create the sort of world we know God believes in; we need a new perspective, unclouded and inspirational.

So as we step into Lent let us be persuaded to try a little gymnastics by placing one foot in each camp. Let us place one foot firmly in the desert and dare to face our devil, in whatever form that comes to us. And let us stand with our other foot firmly on some mountain top breathing in the glory of God. And let us hear again the good news that God's transfiguring love is greater than any evil we can ever imagine.

Part Two

Conversations with a Stranger
Holy Week and the Easter Season

Bethany – a hospitable place

What has Bethany to tell us about the art of hospitality? The village of Bethany, mentioned in the Gospels, may suggest to us themes for our own hospitality – both offered and received, our intentions and dedication. And when it comes to the making of a home, the building of a community, the nurturing and sustenance of a family, what might we glean from that particular home in Bethany that Jesus often frequented?

Bethany, on the top of the Mount of Olives, held a panoramic view of the city of Jerusalem and the desert around it. The slope of the hill was used as a burial ground, and the descent was winding and steep. The Kidron Brook murmured its presence at the base of the hill, as it wound its way past the Garden of Gethsemane.

The disciples and the donkeys would know the journey to Bethany well. They would be glad of the Kidron for the refreshment it offered, counteracting the effects of the strong midday sun. As they journeyed up the Mount they would stop halfway, to get their breath back, thankful for the respite offered by a more level place. They would pause, view the city and steady their knees for the next haul.

In the experience of Jesus, Bethany played an important part. It was away from the noise of the city (though you could hear it rising from below and know its demands). For him, it became an intimate, domestic and significant house and village, for we discover in the Bethany stories something of the very human Jesus – his need for friendship, quiet, a place to belong, to be understood, to be encouraged and blessed. In the days between Palm Sunday and Good Friday, Bethany became vital to him as a place where he could clear the mind – a holy place in Holy Week.

Bethany – a place of welcome. Luke 10.38–42; John 12.1, 2

Here is a house of honesty – a place of delight and disagreement; where a welcome is for no other reason than itself. Here there are no strings attached, no condition-al acceptance, no demands being placed. Here companions encounter one another again in conversation and in breaking bread together.

> Through the chaos, frustration and unpredictability of our living,
> may ordinary, unpretentious and genuine hospitality
> find a home in our lives.

Bethany – a place of anointing. Matthew 26.6–13; Mark 14.3–15; John 12.3–8

The old psalm says, 'You anoint my head with oil' – soothing, healing, significant, personal, gentle, honouring. Here, far beyond words, love is demonstrated. Here is an action that is 'done for my burial' – an action to reach the deepest place of death, loneliness and fear. 'You anoint my head with oil – in the presence of my enemies.' The anointing, reaching to his soul, enables Jesus to enter Jerusalem, to challenge and to save.

> Give us grace always to bless each other in your name,
> for we cannot measure the meaning of such things,
> nor overstate their importance.

Bethany – a place of familiarity. Luke 19.28–36

Jesus had trodden the path many times, he knew the route and could walk it in his imagination; he knew every twist of the journey, the scent of the flowers, the dust in the nostrils, the inhabitants gossiping at the side of the road.

> In our desire for novelty,
> in our insatiable appetite for entertainment,
> in our craving for new experiences,
> may we not denigrate the familiar,
> nor pour scorn on the mundane,
> but be thankful for the places that anchor us,
> the people who hold us safe.

Bethany – a place of rest. Matthew 21.17

Action, anger, debate, hunger, questions, his integrity questioned and the crowds pressing in – and as the tension mounts and the stage is set for the final act, Jesus senses the moment to step aside, to draw breath and seek strength for what was to come.

> Give us the sensitivity to know in our own bodies the rhythm of life –
> rest of the mind,
> rest of the body,
> rest of the heart,
> and rest of the spirit.
> In rest we find renewal and life.

Bethany – a place of resurrection. John 11

An angel with a twinkle in the eye asks a devastating question, 'Why do you seek the living among the dead?' Why indeed? 'He is not here – he is risen.' Resurrection is that moment where death is recognized for what it is and overcome with loving. May every household, every life, every centre of power and responsibility, every place of work, every hungry belly, every violent heart, every inner place of self-awareness, the world itself become a place of resurrection life.

> Each day we awaken to another dawn, another garden, another sunrise:
> give us strength to roll away the stone for each other,
> to loosen bonds with tears and joy.
> Give us courage to bring life out of the tomb, ignoring the stench.

Bethany is still there – a village, donkeys, the vast view, the steep hill, and the first-century tomb, with its weeping chamber. When you visit, 'take off your shoes, for you stand on holy ground'.

For Martha, Mary, Lazarus and Simon, the donkeys and the villagers and all the people of Bethany, we give thanks to God.

Table talk

Gathered around a meal on Maundy Thursday

The following two pieces are suggestions for readings around the meal table on Maundy Thursday.

The first piece might be accompanied by a video projection presenting a montage of images that depict the disparity between the rich and the poor (Christian Aid and CAFOD would have appropriate resources). Each stanza would be read by a different person, seated around the table. Plenty of time should be taken between the reading of each stanza so that people can focus on the images being presented.

This night Jesus offers us a place at the table:

Where we have made it our business to be first in the queue,
as though it were our right;
he asks us to hang back and wait on the generosity of others.

Where we have ensured that the scales would always
be tipped in our favour;
he asks us to empty our pockets and hold out our begging bowl.

Where we have spent too long at table with those who
bolster our image and protect our security;
he asks us to share bread with the excluded and the forgotten.

Where we have 'ummed' and 'aahed', taking too long to choose
from the vast array of food on offer;
he asks us to sit alongside those whose stomachs are rumbling.

This night Jesus offers us a place at the table.

The second piece places the meal within the broader context of the hospitality that marked out Jesus' life and ministry. Space might be given (perhaps before the meal begins) to reflect upon the Hebrew people's concept of hospitality, which Jesus lived to the full, and the influence that those closest to him had upon him.

From whom did you learn the art of hospitality, Jesus?
It seemed to come so naturally to you.
Was it from the one who kick-started you
on to the stage of human history –
was it from Mary?
We watched her at the wedding feast,
always with one eye on the guests,
noticing the empty glass,
aware of someone on their own.
And she kept her eye on you –
'Come on, the wine has run out!'
Did she instil in you the art of extravagant generosity,
of giving without thought of receiving,
of the sheer pleasure of sharing the good things of life?
From whom did you learn the art of hospitality, Jesus?

Thoughts best left unsaid

A meditation on the night of betrayal

Jesus, I hesitate now.
Why are you intent on cutting through the safe image I have of you?
You as the servant of all?
I need you as the figure up front, the decisive leader,
The one behind whom we can all unite.

This humility offends me.
You're asking me to let go,
To rethink my definitions,
To release myself from status,
To relinquish all the norms and the rules
That serve me so well;
You're asking me to act and not to count the cost,
To take the towel and wash the feet,
You're urging me to count as nothing the well-earned place
I've become accustomed to in your kingdom.

I believe in your kingdom come on earth –
But has it really come to this?
Is it I who will betray you?
I feel your kiss of love in the sharing of bread;
But will my kiss smack of bitterness,
Resentment, that I have been stripped of my little bit of power?

You say this feast is open to all;
You say your life is given for all –
Poured out for all –
My head spins at the giddy depths of a love that will not discriminate,
That refuses to make conditions.
I cannot live like that.
I need my boundaries –

I need to know who to love, who to avoid.
I've found my place, here,
Comfortable amid those with whom I rub shoulders,
And wouldn't ask for it any other way.

'Every time you share this feast, remember me.'
'This is my broken body' –
Take, handle, touch, drink, feed,
O God, can heaven be so earthy?

I see your eyes glistening now,
With the tears you can't hold back.
Then I too will weep,
Weep for the chaos and the conflict that
Won't subside in me;
Weep for this dark night that obscures your presence
And leaves me stumbling alone;
Weep for this cruel peace that engulfs my unanswered questions
And offers no relief;
Weep for this cup that will not pass by.

On this night

Prayers in the Garden of Gethsemane

Dear Christ,
On this night you stooped to the ground
making yourself vulnerable for those you loved.
Release us from the need to dominate
and may we recognize you in the faces of the weakest.

Dear Christ,
On this night you were intimate in love,
holding close the one who leant on your breast.
Help us to be open to giving and receiving love,
that we might honour in our lives your prayer for us to live as one.

Dear Christ,
On this night you wept as you faced the horror of your future.
We pray for all who are weeping tonight,
for those who fear the future
and for those who are facing their death alone.

Dear Christ,
On this night you knelt alone in silence.
We pray for ourselves in our aloneness –
for those parts of us that cannot be shared with others,
those parts that we hardly dare own ourselves.

Hold us, dear Christ, this night and every night, in your embrace,
Amen

Prayer from the Cross

The following suggestion for prayer, inspired by the words of Christ on the Cross, needs an uncluttered open space where different images and symbols may be placed and where people have room to walk between the various prayer points.

This works well if the space is open for people to come and go as they wish with no spoken input (possibly with quiet, reflective music in the background), simply the opportunity for personal reflection.

In addition to the symbols suggested, each prayer point might also display a crucifixion image from 'The Christ We Share', produced by the Church Mission Society.

Prayer Point 1: I thirst

Symbol   A water jug filled with water; a drinking glass; dead flowers strewn around.

Prayer   I hold in my heart and before Christ
those without access to clean water;
mothers who will walk for miles this day
to find water for their children;
those who will die this night
from water-borne diseases.
Spirit of Christ,
cascading water of life,
flow freely through this parched world,
and give me a thirst for your justice,
Amen.

To ponder   Jesus' thirst was for all to discover fullness of life. What does that mean for me? Is the thirst that is within me one that compels me toward or distracts me away from the living God?

Action   Take a sip of water.

Prayer Point 2: My God, my God, why have you abandoned me?

Symbol   Two plain masks, devoid of facial expression (available from craft shops and art stores). A basket of miniature masks with paints alongside.

Prayer   I hold in my heart and before Christ
those who find themselves abandoned
and who have lost faith with humanity –
for the abused, the bullied, the victimized;
for those who live out their days in a place that is alien to them.

To ponder   Think of a time when you have been dependent on your own inner resources alone to get you through. What were those resources? Do you value them now? Have you experience of abandonment? If so, how has that influenced your relationship with God? Where do you fear abandonment in your life at present?

Action   Paint a small mask and take it away with you.

Prayer Point 3: Forgive them – they have no idea what they are doing

Symbol   Newspaper cuttings from contemporary events both trivial and profound from around the world. Graffiti board and pen.

Prayer   I hold in my heart and before Christ
this absurd cocktail of images and words;
this snapshot in time of my world.
How it fits together I do not know.
Spirit of Christ,
let me not give way to cynicism,
but travel with me
as I search for missing pieces in the puzzle,
and move painstakingly toward your truth.

To ponder   Reflect on contemporary news headlines. What has been your reaction? What has angered you? What has bored you? What has offended you? What has shocked you? What has brought a smile to your face?

Action   Write a word, phrase or question upon the graffiti board that has come to you at this prayer point.

Prayer Point 4: Today you will be with me in paradise

Symbol   Several large, lit candles of varying height. A basket full of short candles and a large bowl full of sand.

Prayer   I hold in my heart and before Christ
those who will breathe their last breath this day.
I pray especially for . . . . who is close to death.
For those who fear their death, I pray.
For all whose death will be untimely, I pray.
For those whose death will pass unnoticed, I pray.
Spirit of Christ,
bearer of pain,
bring peace and perfect healing
to those who this day will pass from death to life.

To ponder   Recall someone you have known and loved, who has died. Give thanks for the impact her/his life has had upon yours; remember all that his/her living has taught you about the goodness of life and give thanks for the memories.

Action   Light a candle and place it in the sand bowl as you remember, in love, the person in your heart.

Prayer Point 5: It is finished

Symbol   A large egg timer; a tree trunk showing the rings of the tree.

Prayer   I like endings,
I like things to be finished off,
dealt with,
filed away,
neat.
But this is not finished, Lord –
too many crosses still disfigure the horizon,
too many hands still pinned to the wood,

too many hearts still crushed in pain.
When will it be finished?

To ponder These words from the Cross reflect the author's theological interpretation of Jesus' death, believing that the action of God in Christ at this point mysteriously contributes to the redemption of the world. What is your reaction to the Cross of Christ? Where does it intersect with your life? Consider the following extract taken from *Peter Abelard*, Helen Waddell's novel of a medieval love story. Here Abelard and Thibault have stumbled across a rabbit, shrieking in pain in the poacher's trap. Thibault releases it and as it dies in his arms he says,

'. . . all this', he stroked the limp body, 'is because of us. But all the time God suffers. More than we do.'

Abelard looked at him, perplexed. 'Thibault, do you mean Calvary?'

Thibault shook his head. 'That was only a piece of it – the piece we saw – in time. Like that.' He pointed to a fallen tree beside them, sawn through the middle. 'That dark ring there, it goes up and down the whole length of the tree. But you only see it where it is cut across. That is what Christ's life was; the bit of God that we saw. And we think God is like that because Christ was like that, kind, and forgiving sins and healing people. We think that God is like that for ever, because it happened once, with Christ. But not the pain. Not the agony at the last. We think that stopped.'

'Then, Thibault,' Abelard said slowly, 'you think that all this,' he looked down at the little quiet body in his arms, 'all the pain of the world, was Christ's cross?'

'God's cross', said Thibault. 'And it goes on.'

Helen Waddell, *Peter Abelard*, The Reprint Society 1950, pp. 268–70

Action Turn the egg timer over and remain in prayer until all the sand has flowed into the bottom of the timer.

Prayer Point 6: Into your hands I place my spirit

Symbol   Burning incense; a large pile of small blank cards.

Prayer   Can your hands bear the weight of these days?
Can your hands bear the burden of the years?
Do your hands still bear the marks of crucifixion;
    the pain of the world,
    the horror of our inhumanity?
O Christ,
stretch out your hands,
hold this world
    and hold me
in your everlasting embrace.

To ponder   Consider the person you are, the various roles that you live out, the relationships you have, how you define yourself. Write each description down on a separate card. Place your cards in order of significance for you, with the one that carries most weight at the top. Spend time focusing on each, gradually letting go of each role, relinquishing it. When you have been through all the cards focus on what is left. This is the essential core 'you' to be valued and to be offered back to God.

Action   Tear up your cards into tiny pieces and place in the bowl in front of the incense.

Prayers and acclamations for the Easter season

Roll back the stone!
   Let hardness of heart be melted
   in the passion of love.
Roll back the stone!
   Let a cold, clenched fist
   relax into an outstretched hand.
Roll back the stone!
   Let the tentative, tumbling steps
   dance light-footed on the grave.
Roll back the stone for Christ is risen.
  Alleluia!

Dear Jesus,
you call us like Mary Magdalene
to be your companion,
to share your hospitality,
to stand alongside you in the suffering of the world.
May we recognize your voice inviting us to let go
   of all that would hold us back;
so with hands free,
we may embrace your resurrection life,
Amen

God gives us this new day
Amen! We claim its potential.
God offers us a new beginning
Amen! We affirm resurrection.
God beckons us to an ever open future
Amen! We take our next step.
Let us go in love
Giving thanks to God!

The table is set

A eucharistic prayer for the Easter season

God is in our midst!
Her spirit is with us!
Let us lift up our hearts!
Let us lift them in song!
Let us celebrate God's limitless presence!
Let us rejoice in God's unending love!

Jesus, your table is set, your feast is ready
and in your love there is space for us here.
Your outstretched hands beckon us,
your open heart welcomes us,
your resurrection life compels us
and we are drawn to you.

The table is set, the feast is now ready,
let all find a place in God's love.

Jesus, your table is set, your feast is ready
yet we know there are empty places;
we know that through division and betrayal
not all find a welcome at your banquet,
not all find a seat at your table.
So call the broken, the despairing, the hungry,
the dispossessed, the lonely, the dying –
all who have been excluded.

Call in the name of love,
that God's house may be full!
Call in the name of life,
that resurrection may be sung!
Call in the name of hope,
that the dance of life may
echo through this universe!

Jesus, you sat at table with friend and betrayer alike.
You blessed the cup and shared the bread
and asked to be remembered.
You blessed the cup and shared the bread
and wept your tears of love.
You blessed the cup and shared the bread
and stared into the abyss of death and destruction.

Kyrie eleison
Christe eleison
Kyrie eleison

Yet death could not contain you,
fear could not restrain you,
hatred and enmity could not have the final say.
And today we celebrate your life
Praise God!
Today we celebrate your love
Praise God!
Today we celebrate your joy
for we are a people of hope
Praise God!
We announce resurrection in our lives,
in this place and in the life of our world.
So pervade this feast with the life of your Spirit,
and free us to be your people of hope.

The table is set, the feast is now ready,
let all find a place in God's love.

We break this bread remembering the brokenness of the world;
Yes, we will remember.
We raise this cup celebrating the sign of God's presence among us;
Yes, we celebrate God's love.

The Lord's Prayer is said

The table is set, the feast is now ready,
come, find a place in God's love.

Communion is shared

Why do you look for the living among the dead?

Thoughts on Easter Day

Have you seen the film *The Shawshank Redemption*? It contains a particularly memorable scene where the main character, Andy, in prison for allegedly killing his wife, is sifting through the books in the prison library. Due to his striking personality and sense of presence, Andy has been put in charge of the library. One day he comes across an old recording of Mozart's *The Marriage of Figaro*, and while the guard is distracted Andy locks the door, puts the record on the player, flicks on the prison sound system and out flows the most beautiful music that permeates across the hard, dark world of the prison compound.

And all over the yard men in prison uniforms gradually raise their heads, as the music surges over the bleak, institutional space and into their souls. The eyes of some of the men become moist as for four minutes they find themselves transformed, transported beyond their limited world into a moment of pure release and freedom. The narrator in the film likens the music to that of some beautiful bird that had descended into the men's drab little cage, making the hard, black walls dissolve away – and for the briefest moment every last man at Shawshank prison felt he had stepped into new life and was free.

During the Easter season we will talk much in our churches of new life, of resurrection life, of the power of life to overcome death. But how seriously do we believe it? And where might we be seeking it?

For Jesus resurrection from the dead was what he believed in passionately. The way he lived his life, every breath he breathed, every word he spoke, was a step toward resurrection. That was what characterized his ministry. To the woman who had had life drained out of her, oppressed by moral and religious codes, Jesus says, 'Daughter . . . go in peace.' To the disciple distraught and guilt-ridden following his denial of Christ, Jesus poses the challenge, 'Do you love me? . . . then follow me.' To the little man shunned by society because of his trade, Jesus says, 'Come here and let me dine with you.' His every waking moment was concerned with the transmission of life to those who had settled, or been forced to settle, for partly living. And given all of that, Jesus' own coming back to life on the third day was surely the affirmation of how he had lived every moment of every day.

I have long been intrigued by the way in which artists through the centuries have depicted the resurrection; in particular I have noted the way in which the Orthodox Church seems to place an emphasis on the sheer effort involved in the movement from death to life. Unlike some of the paintings emerging from the Western Church (where moving the boulder at the entrance of the tomb can at times appear to pose no more of a challenge to the risen Christ than flicking a crumb across the table), paintings from the Orthodox tradition somehow capture more of a sense of the enormous effort, strength and great cost involved in this passionate thrust toward new life.

And what of us? Are we a part of this thrust toward life, toward fullness of living, toward resurrection in the here and now, or have we got stuck into a mode of half living? Do we continue to look for the living among the dead? 'Give a man an all-day breakfast and a squidgy pillow and watch him sleep his way through life' is a remark I heard some years ago that has stayed with me. Most people in this country will spend an average of three years of their life watching television commercials alone. Do we really believe in resurrection? Do we really believe that the fullness of life is possible in the here and now?

A cursory glance around our churches at present might well indicate that Christians no longer believe in the reality of resurrection – nodding in ascent to the historic credal formularies of the Church seems as far as many Christians are pre-pared to go. Onlookers at the Church may get a sense that Christians are more at home in the garden of remembrance than the garden of resurrection. Often it seems the Church is clinging to structures, systems, even words that no longer mediate the living God, because they have become substitutes for God and not channels through which God can impart new life.

The story goes of a woman out walking her dog one afternoon. She crosses a field and notices two men standing in the middle of it; both with a spade in their hands. As she got close to them she noticed that one was digging a hole with his spade and placing the earth at the side of it while the other appeared to be shovelling up the discarded earth and placing it back in the hole. Intrigued by this, the woman addressed the two men, asking, 'Can you explain to me what you are doing?' 'Well, it's like this,' said the man digging the hole, 'I'm Tom whose job it is to dig the hole, then there's Dick who places the tree in the hole, and then there's Harry who secures the tree by filling up the hole with the earth. . . . except Dick's off sick today.'

Mark Oakley, speaking at a national conference of the Retreat Association, urged our churches to become 'Gymnasiums of the Divine'. What a lovely metaphor! How can we create spaces for the divine presence to take our breath away? How can we encourage others to live in a spirit of expectancy as God, the acrobat, tumbles, spins, balances, soars? How do we learn the art of mirroring this playful, joyful, creative activity of God in our midst – a God whose energy and delight inspires us to step beyond the grave into the very fullness of life?

Why do you look for the living among the dead? The question posed two thousand years ago is still ringing in our ears. May God grant us the courage and the desire to take hold of life and live resurrection to the full.

Conversations with a stranger

Thoughts on Luke 24.13–35

To my mind, the account of the conversation along the road to Emmaus has got to be one of the most fascinating stories about Jesus recorded in the Bible.

According to Luke (and also indicated in Mark), this encounter takes place within hours of the resurrection and the first reports that something highly unusual might have taken place. Our two disciples are clearly aware of the latest developments, but seem at a loss as to what to make of them. Surely we can forgive them this – after all, which of us would react any differently if we were told that someone close to us who we knew was certified dead and buried had been seen alive and (seemingly) well two days later? We'd be inclined to think that the heat was getting to them a bit! Moreover, the last thing any of us would be remotely prepared for would be for the said dead-and-buried friend to saunter up to us on the road and start having a chat! I wonder what was going through their minds . . . 'Has anyone ever told you you look like . . .' 'Yeah, the likeness is amazing, you could be his twin . . .' 'Galilean accent as well – remarkable . . .' and knowing what they knew, it just might have crossed their minds – 'Maybe . . . just possibly . . . could it be . . .? Nah, don't be daft!' And even if they were remotely tempted to think it just might be more than Jesus' double, they, like any of us, would be inclined to dismiss the possibility out of hand – it must be the heat getting to them! Or the grief and stress of an unbelievable few days . . .

So, while it seems incredible to us that they wouldn't recognize Jesus, if we think ourselves into their situation, it's perfectly reasonable that they might not. Then again, they were also so preoccupied with what had happened that, when this strangely familiar figure with a strangely familiar voice starts questioning them in a strangely familiar way, they don't stop to think – 'Hey, that's strangely familiar' – they're too occupied with what's going on in their own heads to look beyond the end of their noses. And even as he engages them in deep conversation, and enables them to pour out their hearts about what's happening (now, who used to do that quite a lot?), and even explains to them the meaning of much of what they're talking about, the penny still does not drop.

But Jesus continues to journey on with them, even to the point of agreeing to stay and eat with them. And then Mr Strangely-Familiar performs a strangely familiar action. He takes the bread, he says a blessing, he breaks it and he passes it to them. And now they recognize him! I've often wondered what the 'tipping point' was – what took them from almost not daring to believe it to suddenly realizing that . . . 'Yes, no, it can't be . . . but it is! It really is! It's him!!!' Was it the blessing he gave? Was it the manner in which he broke the bread, not entirely dissimilar to what they may well have seen happen in an upper room just days earlier? Or could it be that, as he physically breaks bread and passes it into their hands, his sleeves fall back and his wounds are revealed? That might well 'tip the balance', just as it did for Thomas later on. Jesus is recognized, not only in the symbolic breaking of his body, but in the reality of the wounds of crucifixion on the hands that reach out to them! 'Jesus – it really is you, isn't it . . . isn't it? Jesus?'

But at their point of recognition and acknowledgement, Jesus disappears. One can imagine these two disciples, now just the two of them, still holding the piece of bread that, seconds earlier, they received from the wounded hand of Jesus, looking gog-eyed at one another across the table, shaking with fear, excitement, joy, bewilderment . . . 'I didn't imagine that, did I . . . no . . . it really was him . . . Aha! Now it makes sense – all that stuff he was saying out on the road – I knew it, I knew it – oh boy, c'mon, we need to get back to Jerusalem . . .'

And so, having so recently trudged wearily along the road, they turn tail and hurtle back to Jerusalem to find the other disciples and tell them what has happened. And, if Mark's Gospel is correct, they got pretty much the same response that they themselves had given on hearing earlier reports of Jesus' resurrection – Mark 16.13: 'And they went back and told the rest, but they did not believe them.'

Why might this story be important? One reason I'd like to suggest is that it's almost a kind of 'blueprint' for the way that the risen Christ 'walks humbly' ever onwards alongside those he loves – whether they claim to know him and love him or not!

The resurrection takes place – then what? What does Jesus do next? He's back on the road, journeying again with those he loves. And you could say he's been doing it ever since – that journey, begun on the road to Emmaus, continues to this day, as Christ continues to draw alongside people – some who know him, many who don't; some who've 'known him for years' without ever realizing who he really is, others who weren't remotely expecting him, or maybe haven't yet realized he's in their midst. Some don't know his name, and maybe, in their lifetimes, won't know his name, but welcome him alongside them and he gladly joins them; there are others who say they don't want his company thank-you-very-much, but to whom he remains unobtrusively near. He jogs briskly with those who want to run, while sharing in the slow, painful steps of others. And his love compels him even to stand with those who refuse to budge, but with the ever-present, gentle encouragement to 'come'.

But the Bible testifies that it isn't really in God's nature to stand still – from

Abraham departing for the Promised Land, to the tribes of Israel on their journey through the desert, to the missionary exploits of the early Church and beyond, God has always wanted to be on the move with his people – not just because of his love for them and desire to be with them, but because our God is a pilgrim God, a God who journeys onwards. And I wonder if that innate need to journey is a characteristic of God in us!

And what can we learn of ourselves from the two disciples? Their preoccupations prevented them from looking beyond the end of their noses – how often can we fall into that trap? Moreover, they were not, at first, ready to have the risen Christ journey with them – maybe we can hardly blame them for that, but, ready or not, Jesus was there and, in his own time, he allowed them to become aware of his identity. But, to their credit, they welcomed the stranger alongside them regardless and shared their lives, and their food, with him. Hebrews 13.2 offers this intriguing thought: 'Do not neglect to show hospitality to strangers, for by doing that some have entertained angels without knowing it.' As we journey on, in the knowledge of God's desire to journey with us, are we also ready to welcome the stranger – in whatever form he or she takes – alongside us on the road?

And finally, let's remember how Jesus ultimately revealed himself to those disciples: not only in the symbolic demonstration of his sacrifice, but in the physical evidence of his love and commitment – the wounds on his hands. Maybe a final challenge is not only to be aware of the stranger alongside us on our journey, but ourselves to be that stranger alongside others on theirs, revealing as we go the love of Christ that opens eyes and lifts hearts. Christ is recognized by the disciples in the signs of self-giving love. And so he is recognized in us when we seek to do as he did and express the love of God to the world around us. So may God bless us all as we journey on from here, on our individual paths, as we journey together and as we walk with our pilgrim God to every corner of creation.

The feast of life

Thoughts on Luke 14.1–24

Luke 14.1–24

He said also to the one who had invited him, 'When you give a luncheon or a dinner, do not invite your friends or your brothers or your relatives or rich neighbours, in case they may invite you in return, and you would be repaid. But when you give a banquet, invite the poor, the crippled, the lame, and the blind. And you will be blessed, because they cannot repay you, for you will be repaid at the resurrection of the righteous.'

I used to live in a residential community in Milton Keynes – there were 15 of us who were attempting the phenomenally difficult task of sharing our lives together. But amid much that was difficult there was one aspect we always celebrated – that of food! Due to the culinary skills of one particular member of our community, we frequently sat down together to feast on the most delicious meals. As a community we were called 'The Well' and occasionally we'd joke about changing our name to the 'Eat Well' Community, because we always did. And once a month on a Friday evening we held a spectacular feast; we called it the 'Open Table' and offered an open invitation to all – anyone who wanted to join us was welcome at the table. Sometimes a visitor would take the floor and share something of particular interest or concern to him/her; other evenings the meal itself was all it took for people to engage with one another and share of themselves. And just occasionally, gathered around that open table, in the conversations, the banter, the gossip, the reaching out to one another, we'd get a sense that perhaps we weren't too far from Christ's feast of life. In the disagreements, the food, the laughter, the welcome, occasionally we'd catch a whiff of God's intoxicating generosity being shared among us.

In our Gospel story, we hear that Jesus went to eat in the house of a prominent Pharisee (presumably he'd been invited and wasn't simply gatecrashing). In the home there was a man who was disabled – partially paralysed; it was the holy day so Jesus asks them all what they think of breaking a tradition and healing on their sacred day. The response he gets is one of embarrassed silence – they look down at their toes, and someone conveniently sneaks off to get the starter. The rest shuffle around with the seating arrangements and gradually, one by one, they begin to take their places, with a distinctly bad taste in their mouths – even before any food has been eaten. Jesus lets pass the opportunity to enquire who his neighbours are on either side of him – how far they've travelled, what they do for a living, the sort of polite chitchat we're all well versed in. Instead he opts for launching into a blistering attack on his host, by criticizing the seating arrangements and suggesting his host should have invited a completely different crowd altogether. Someone (and it sounds quite typical of Peter) tries to save the day by stuffing the silence full of an irrelevant one-liner: 'O blessed is the one who will eat in the kingdom of God!' But Jesus is having none of it and promptly embarks on the parable of the Great Feast.

So typical of Jesus! He loved a good meal – he was always eating and, whenever he did, he never missed the opportunity to let it speak of the things of God, the way life is in God's kingdom. Do you remember him in Matthew's house where society's rejects sense his acceptance of them and dare to join him in a meal? Inevitably mumblings and criticisms are heard around him and Jesus responds by saying that perhaps those sitting at table with him are more in need of his company than those, as John Bell so eloquently put it, pickled in self-righteousness. He lunches with a Pharisee who happens to notice he hasn't ritually washed his hands before eating. What's his reply: 'O sorry, I forgot, I'll go and do it now'? No! It is more like, 'You fools, try to be a bit more concerned about what's going on on the inside, not the outside.' Even a grain of wheat, being eaten nonchalantly by his disciples as they passed through a cornfield, became the focus of a conversation around living lives of integrity.

Where have you seen the feast of life celebrated recently? Where have you witnessed Christ's banquet being shared this last week in your own locality? If you have trouble identifying it, let me offer you three helpful hints that might enable you to recognize it this coming week.

First, as our Gospel story reminds us, the feast is likely to be discovered where the seating arrangements have been abolished, where there has been no careful thought given as to who are the acceptable guests; where there's no sense of 'them' and 'us', where each person is open to receiving the food of life from his or her neighbour, no matter who they are, where they've come from, what they look like. Perhaps that's why we don't find ourselves part of the feast of life too often, for if we're honest, we all like our boundary markers – we make snap judgements about people within seconds, we subconsciously enter Harry Potter's world and subject others to Dumbledore's sorting hat the moment we meet them. It's safer for us that way – we're less likely to feel threatened and more likely to be able to remain within the security of our own comfort zone. And it's not just on a one to one basis that we behave like this, but so too as a nation we need to know who's out and who's in, we need our scapegoats, be it Muslims, asylum seekers, paedophiles, the mentally ill. Our seating arrangements provide us with assurance that no undesirables get in; we're in control, we're safe, for we know with whom we're dealing.

Yet Christ calls us to a more risky lifestyle. He asks to step out beyond the comfortable and the familiar; he asks us to go with nothing in our hands save an openness to what and who we might encounter. He asks us to look and see himself reflected in the eyes of others, recognizing that it is precisely those from whom we might instinctively recoil who are most likely to be God's gift to us. God asks us to welcome the outsider, the labelled, the dispossessed at our own tables, taking leaps of faith for the sake of love.

Where else might you look to discover the feast of life? Well, it's likely to be 'out there'. Jesus was always 'going on his way', a phrase that's considered by some scholars to be simply a linking device between different narratives, but which I think makes an important theological statement – Jesus was always going on his way, sharing the feast of life beyond the so-called holy places. Think of the woman with whom he conversed outside the village, beside the well, cut off from the hubbub of village life; think of the dialogue with a repentant thief on a public hill, not in the temple; think of the little man, society's reject, sat in the tree away from the flow of the crowd, to whom Jesus gave his time and with whom he chose to eat.

When I was in parish ministry I recall being approached by a woman who lived just up the road, asking me if there might be someone from the church who could sit with her severely disabled son for an hour or two every so often, so that she could get a bit of space for herself. I told her I would ask around and see what was possible (feeling guilty that I had not volunteered myself). My first approach was to the pastoral care group, but there was no joy there. I then gave out the notice for several weeks each Sunday morning at the main service – nobody took up the offer. Then one Sunday afternoon there was frantic knocking on my vicarage door. The mother of the child was beside herself with fear and worry: her son was nowhere to be found, please could I help her search for him? Six of us scoured the neighbourhood for the best part of an hour. Eventually we found him – he was sat in a large caravan at the side of the road, one of a convoy in which a number of travellers lived. He was among a family. All were drinking tea and playing cards. My neighbour's son had been given a plastic beaker which enabled him to drink too. He had a huge smile on his face; it was evident to all he was having the time of his life.

Christ's feast of life is being shared this very day in unexpected places, among unsuspecting people. Christ's banquet is being spread out this very moment in the most unlikely nooks and crannies, and we are asked to keep our eyes wide open, always on the lookout for where God's food is being shared. We're asked to keep our hearts wide open so that we can join in and celebrate God's hospitality wherever it is evident. God calls and coaxes us, inviting us to move beyond our holy huddles, our churches and chapels, for the bread of life has got to be broken in the street as well as in the sanctuary, broken and shared, again and again and again.

And finally, if you want another clue as to where the feast of life is being celebrated, it is to be found wherever you or I or anyone recognizes a need for God and takes a step in the direction of life. Like those in Jesus' parable we can be full of excuses – we've a holiday to sort, a business to run, a lottery ticket to buy, and we rush through life unaware of the fullness of life that is there for the taking; unaware of the feast that is spread out, if only we'd stop and be attentive. When Jesus met the Samaritan woman at the well what was his plea to her? 'If only you knew what God is offering you', were his words to her. 'You come to this well every day to draw your water and yet you're not in touch with the God of life.' And we may come to church every Sunday, but do we really taste the feast of life? Do we know what God is offering us? Has our religion, however it is expressed, become a substitute for engaging with the living God? John Taylor in his beautiful book *The Go-between God* (SCM, 1972) suggests that God's offer of life 'so far exceeds the petty scale we want to live by. He has made us little lower than gods, while our highest ambition is to be a little above the Joneses. We are looking for a sensible, 'family size' God, dispensing pep-pills or tranquilizers as required, with a Holy Spirit who is a baby's comforter.' 'If only you knew what God is offering', says Christ to us. The Church is so busy squeezing its dreams into dogma, its visions into orthodoxy that it has forgotten what it feels like to be caressed by the breath and play of God's Spirit. We go through the motions, through the ritual, and our sharing of the feast of life can become a mockery of the extravagant love of God's grace poured out in our world.

As we break bread and share wine together in a moment, dare we dream our dreams and broaden our vision? Will our sharing at our eucharistic tables force us out to see the world with eyes wide open? And in meeting with one another at the table will we be able to move beyond the limitations, the boundaries, the belief systems that ultimately divide person from person? Have we got it in us to step beyond the cosy, privatized religion (where we rub along with the people sitting next to us in the pew) that is such a far cry from living out Christ's radical rule of love and hospitality within our world? Do we, in the end, have vision enough to see our own tables as a foretaste of the great heavenly banquet? Dare we be extravagant in the name of love?

Pray God that we might.

Extravagant love

A liturgy for corporate prayer in the morning

The words printed in bold are to be said by all.

To be alive this day
This is your gift to me!
To breathe and stretch and yawn
This is your life in me!
To step into this day with you at my side
This is your faith in me!

Your presence fills the universe
yet you choose to lodge here, within me.
You are beyond my wildest imaginings
yet you are closer than my very own breath.
I know you in the smile of the stranger, in the tear of a child,
yet you are as elusive as the wave on the shore.
God of mystery and delight,
God of tenderness and longing,
nurture your life within me,
that I may be free in you,
Amen

Song / Music

Dear Christ,
in the moments when I don't know where to turn
and forget that you are my pole star:
help me to turn to you.

In the moments when I am lonely
and forget that you are my companion:
help me to remember that you are beside me.

In the moments when I weep
and forget that your eyes glisten with tears:
help me to sense your sharing in the pain.

In the moments when my friends surround me
yet I fail to see your image reflected:
help me to see you in their eyes.

In the moments when I laugh
yet fail to trust the music in my soul:
help me to hear the echo of your life within me.

In all of these moments,
strange and joyful, beautiful and challenging,
happy and despairing:
help me to remember your presence.

Reading

Reflection (silent or spoken)

Prayers for the day
Using the following words or as led by the leader

> Consider the lilies of the field,
> they neither toil nor spin,
> yet even Solomon in all his glory
> was not clothed like one of these.
>
> Matthew 6.28–29

So taken up with all we must do,
all we must be,
all we must achieve,
we pray, dear Christ, for ourselves in all our complexity;
teach us to stop and stare;
to stand empty-handed before you;
to drink deeply from the well of your love
and know ourselves accepted.

Silence

Who will separate us from the love of Christ?
Will hardship, or distress, or persecution?

Romans 8.35

We pray today for all who will trip themselves up;
for those buckling under the stress of demands
and responsibilities;
for those who can no longer hold it together;
for those who are putting on a brave face.

Silence

When I look at the heavens, the work of your fingers,
the moon and the stars that you have established;
what are human beings that you are mindful of them,
mortals that you care for them?

Psalm 8.3, 4

We pray today for those who have lost a sense of self-worth,
for those who cannot value themselves
and who doubt your faith in them.
We pray for those who cannot wipe the slate clean
and yet who long to start again.

Prayers may continue either spoken or silent

We offer all our prayers through Christ,
Amen

A prayer for the work of the day may be offered

The Lord's Prayer may be said

Song / Music

And now,
as we go on our way,
may nothing we say or do
contradict these thoughts and prayers,

offered today
in integrity and faith.

We go in the name of Christ!
Thanks be to God!

We go on our way living out the hospitality of God.

Part Three

In God's Company
Ordinary Time in Summer and Autumn

Moses, what did you witness?

An active meditation

The following active meditation is based on an evening worship service led by members of the Scargill Community at the annual Greenbelt Festival. It can be adapted as a Lenten meditation, using the desert as the primary focus. Alternatively, this could be offered as a meditation to coincide with Human Rights Day or Remembrance Sunday.

Aim: Taking the biblical reading of Moses in the desert as the backdrop, this active meditation invites us to step into the desert places of our present day and age, to recall and pray for those whose lives are diminished through war, bloodshed, persecution and fear.

You will need

- A very large plastic sheet covered in sand – some of which will need to be damp in order for sandcastles to be made. *(Please note: a lot of sand is needed for this meditation to be effective!)*
- Pieces of debris, e.g. the sort of items that are washed up on a beach or lie around a garden
- Paper and pencils for all participants
- Facts and figures concerning the plight of children in the world, clearly printed on different cards. *(These facts can be obtained through the charity Save the Children.)* In addition, stories taken from newspaper articles might sit alongside the facts and figures
- Three or four buckets and spades
- A selection of candles
- CD player

Setting up the space

- Participants will be seated either on the floor or on chairs around the edge of the 'desert space'

- Pieces of debris are sticking out of the sand. *(It is important to ensure that this can be clearly seen so that nobody is likely to trip over anything.)*
- A bowl with paper and pens and a bowl with a selection of candles are placed in the sand and are clearly visible to all
- The cards and cuttings with facts and figures will be placed in the sand, randomly
- The buckets and spades will be placed at obvious points in the sand

The active meditation begins with the following words from Exodus 3.1–12:

> Moses was keeping the flock of his father-in-law Jethro, the priest of Midian; he led his flock beyond the wilderness, and came to Horeb, the mountain of God. There the angel of the LORD appeared to him in a flame of fire out of a bush; he looked, and the bush was blazing, yet it was not consumed. Then Moses said, 'I must turn aside and look at this great sight, and see why the bush is not burned up.' When the LORD saw that he had turned aside to see, God called to him out of the bush, 'Moses, Moses!' And he said, 'Here I am.' Then he said, 'Come no closer! Remove the sandals from your feet, for the place on which you are standing is holy ground.' He said further, 'I am the God of your father, the God of Abraham, the God of Isaac, and the God of Jacob.' And Moses hid his face, for he was afraid to look at God.
>
> Then the LORD said, 'I have observed the misery of my people who are in Egypt; I have heard their cry on account of their taskmasters. Indeed, I know their sufferings, and I have come down to deliver them from the Egyptians, and to bring them up out of that land to a good and broad land, a land flowing with milk and honey, to the country of the Canaanites, the Hittites, the Amorites, the Perizzites, the Hivites, and the Jebusites. The cry of the Israelites has now come to me; I have also seen how the Egyptians oppress them. So come, I will send you to Pharaoh to bring my people, the Israelites, out of Egypt.' But Moses said to God, 'Who am I that I should go to Pharaoh, and bring the Israelites out of Egypt?' He said, 'I will be with you; and this shall be the sign for you that it is I who sent you: when you have brought the people out of Egypt, you shall worship God on this mountain.'

Voice 1   *(shouted)* If you have eyes to see, then look!

Pause

Moses, what did you witness in the midst of the arid desert?
A bush ablaze? What did you see amid the flames?
Your people emblazoned in a furnace?
Your people crying out to be set free?

Pause

Voice 2 Come, let us step into that desert place too. See the bush still ablaze.
   Take a look, today and through the years. Stare into
      the ovens of Auschwitz,
        the genocide of Rwanda,
         the desperation of Darfur,
          the devastation of Iraq.
   If you have eyes to see, then look!

As appropriate music is played people are invited to walk around the 'desert' strewn with debris, to write their own prayers for peace and place them in the sand

Voice 1 *(shouted)* If you have ears to hear, then listen!

   Pause

   Moses, what did you hear under the night sky of the desert?
   The cries of a people who had long since given up hope?
   The sighs of a people who were no longer able to dream?

   Pause

Voice 2 Come, let us step into that desert place too.
   Hear the eerie silence of
     the absence of laughter
      the abandoned street
       the empty, haunted eyes
        the discarded toy and unstrung guitar.
   If you have ears to hear, then listen!

As appropriate music is played people are invited to read the quotations, the facts and the figures, placed in the sand concerning the plight of children in the world. They are invited to build a sandcastle as a symbol of prayer for those whose dreams have been crushed, for those whose childhoods have ended all too soon

Voice 1 *(shouted)* If you have feet to walk, then journey!

   Pause

   Moses, what compelled you to journey into that desert?
   From whom and from what were you running?

   Pause

Voice 2   Come, let us journey into that desert place too.
           Walk alongside those who are on the move this night:
               those running from fear,
                   hiding from the authorities,
                       seeking a refuge
                           escaping from violence
                               running from their past,
                                   in search of a home.
           If you have feet to walk, then journey!

As appropriate music is played people are invited to leave their footprints in the sand and to light a candle beside them, holding in their hearts and before God all those whose journeys are painful and costly

When all have finished lighting candles people are invited to sit around the edge of the 'desert' and chants are sung. The meditation then concludes with the following prayer:

Dear Christ,
we now leave this desert space,
but we will carry with us
the stark facts laid bare before us,
the insights from others offered around us,
and the yearnings of our souls deep within us.
Keep our eyes open
our ears alert
and our feet ready to journey
for your name's sake.
Amen

Prayers for the Summer season

Amid the sheer beauty of life around us,
we want to hold in our hearts and before you
the pain-filled places of the world
where divisions and injustice scar your image.

Amid the companionship of those around us,
we want to hold in our hearts and before you
the ones who are isolated and fearful
and who long for connection.

Amid the laughter and celebration of life,
we want to hold in our hearts and before you
the ones who are hurting in mind or body
and who have no song to sing.

Amid all that baffles us, confuses us
and causes us to lose our bearings,
we cherish in our hearts and before you
those who love and believe in us.

Christ our Companion,
for all the delights that life holds for us,
for all the wonders that are ours to enjoy
    we thank you.
During this season of holidays and relaxation
we pray especially for those who
    struggle to celebrate life –
those who shoulder too much suffering,
those who have lost faith
    and who fear the future.
Be there for all who need your reassuring presence,
this day and every day.
Amen

The imprint of God

A meditation using clay

Aim: to explore the connections between our creativity, our sensitivity and our spirituality

Each participant is given a lump of clay about the size of a tennis ball, and is seated in front of a table or hard surface upon which to work the clay.

A centrepiece with a pottery jug or potter's wheel with different-sized lumps of clay may aid the meditation. There may be background music while people are working with the clay.

The facilitator will need to be confident in her/his own affinity with clay. The thoughts offered below are some suggestions for exploring the medium of clay; it is hoped these thoughts will spark off other thoughts in the facilitator. Ample space should be given for personal reflection during the meditation and for the sharing of thoughts at the end.

Suggested ideas for a guided meditation

Introductory thoughts about a ball of clay being a minor planet – how the clay came to be – the disintegration of rock through millions of years. Earliest clays deposited 300 million years ago

How do you feel about this clay? Do you like its messiness, its dirtiness? Do you mind dirt? Does it take you back to your childhood? Were you one of those children who were told that 'cleanliness is next to godliness'? Were you allowed to mess around in the dirt?

Invite participants to squeeze their lump of clay then press their thumb into it

The clay is very sensitive – it is reflecting back to you a part of yourself.

Read extracts from Psalm 139

Invite participants to close their eyes and break their lump of clay into two equal-sized balls, then to place one ball in each hand

Note that the work is being done by the body alone – the mind has very little to offer. Be aware of your body at work and the sensitivity of your hands, the weight of the clay within your palms. If you were having to divide something equally, you'd normally reach for a gadget, probably the kitchen scales or a measurement of some description. We fill our lives with gadgets which perhaps in the end have the cumulative effect of making us less sensitive. Think of Jesus' life and the way in which he engaged with others: recall his response to the woman who touched the hem of his garment; his sensitivity to the tired and hungry crowd; his dialogue with the blind men at the side of the road, straining to be heard amid the crowd. Jesus' response was always a testimony to the depth of sensitivity that one person could hold in their being. Perhaps you know others who hold something of that same characteristic within themselves?

Invite participants to make something with their clay

Was the task hard or easy? If it was difficult can you identify what got in the way? Is it possible that voices from the past were commenting, either aiding or criticizing? And how hard a critic is God in your life? Has this always been the case?

Ask participants to squeeze up their creation in clay and then pass it on to the person on their right

The story goes of a miser who found it difficult to let go of anything. One day he fell to the bottom of a deep well. The villagers gathered around wanting to help, each in turn reaching down the well and shouting, 'Give me your hand.' But the miser refused to co-operate. Then from the back of the crowd a woman came forward; she stretched down the well and shouted, 'Here, take my hand', and immediately, at hearing the word 'take', the miser put out his hand and was hauled to safety.

Perhaps there is not very much difference between giving and receiving (except to a miser).

Invite participants to create something with their clay that has no name or defined shape

Was this a difficult or easy task? Naming gives us power over things – think of the creation myths and the naming of every creature by Adam in the garden. Did you experience any powerlessness in creating something you could not easily define?

73

Invite participants to knead the clay like bread and to watch their hands at work

We take our hands for granted and yet they are such a great force in life. We are told that God acted in the Hebrew Scriptures 'with a mighty hand and an out-stretched arm'. By contrast, the man in the Gospel who had a withered hand appears to have had no creative power at all. Why might that be? Again, think of the creation myths and reflect on the connections between creativity and life/energy. The story is told of a dancer who, through her movement, brought to life a group of elderly people. Day after day the elderly residents had sat together in the lounge, with the television blaring out yet with no visible connection to the world or to one another. Through the beauty and creativity of the dance, each person gradually began to come to life, poignant memories began to be evoked, life began to return to their eyes and hands began to stretch out toward one another. To what extent do you avoid coming to life? Is it easier to remain partially alive, existing within a predictable universe?

Invite participants to share their thoughts from the guided meditation

The meditation ends with each member of the group passing their clay to the person on their right. As the clay is passed on the following words are read:

> It is not thou that shapest God;
> it is God that shapeth thee.
> For then thou art the work of God,
> waiting for the hand of the artist
> who does all things in due season.
> Offer him thy heart, soft and tractable,
> and keep the form in which the artist has shapen thee.
> Let the clay be moist,
> lest thou grow hard
> and lose the imprint of his fingers.
>
> Irenaeus

I am grateful to Donagh O'Shea's book, *Go Down Into the Potter's House* (Michael Glazier, 1988), for inspiration for this chapter.

Mary Magdalene: Companion on the way

Celebrating the feast day of this saint, 22 July

Mary Magdalene is a paradox. Many of us would probably claim to know her quite well – a familiar character in the Christian story – and yet, when pushed, we would probably have to confess we know remarkably little. We have no idea as to her initial encounter with Jesus, neither do we know what she had to leave behind in order to embark on an itinerant lifestyle with him. We are not privy to any discourses between her and Jesus, at least not until we reach the point of resurrection and hear that poignant dialogue with the resurrected Christ in the garden. She is simply there, a familiar figure along with a whole group of women who, we are told, provided for Jesus out of their means, offering him and his friends a place of hospitality, a sense of home, as they went on their way.

There's a little book called *The Gospel of Philip* which never made it into the New Testament canon, in which Mary is described as the one who always 'walked with Jesus'; a 'Companion of the Lord'.

And perhaps that is the first indication that Mary is a very contemporary role model for our churches. How much we have to learn from her warm companionship of Christ. A companion is someone with whom, quite literally, you break bread – that is what the word means. Wouldn't it be lovely for our churches to be known as those places where people have learnt the art of warm companionship, safe places where hospitality is the overriding hallmark? Wouldn't it be lovely for our churches to be places where it was evident people simply spent time in Christ's company, breaking bread and sharing his nourishment with those beyond the sacred space? A genuine ministry of unpretentious hospitality – that is what we are all called to, in the name of Christ.

There's a third-century tradition where Mary Magdalene has the distinct reputation of being a questioner. She is said to have asked 39 questions of Jesus and in dialogue says to him, 'I will not tire of asking you. Do not be angry with me for questioning everything.' And Jesus replies, 'Question what you will.' And Jesus' approval surely gives hope to those of us who flinch at that rigid sort of spirituality where conformity to the rules is given higher credence than a questing spirit; where what you believe is of greater significance than why you believe it. This picture of Mary, which equates depth of faith with exploration and an unwillingness to be put down, flies in the face of so much fundamentalist religion today, from which-ever stable it is coming – the sort of religion that frowns on our questions and stamps on our individualism. We know that at least 70 per cent of the people in Britain claim a spirituality and yet feel the Church no longer has the language or the ability to connect with them on their journey. What are the questions that we need to be asking? And when others, especially those on the outside of our churches, begin to formulate the questions, are we listening? Or, out of our own sense of anxiety, are we too quick to offer easy answers? Perhaps we need to learn to resist the seduction of quick clarity, for honest seekers after truth (and there are many out there) are less and less convinced by 'bumper sticker' theology, which may offer immediate relief but does little to address the underlying anxieties and complexities of life. Sometimes I think our churches can sound like broken fax machines – always on transmit, forever giving out the answers but not listening to the ques-tions. And occasionally we trip ourselves up: have you heard about the church in London, for example, that came up with a slick one-liner for the hoarding outside the church which read, 'If you're tired of your sin, then come on in!' – on to which someone had scrawled in red, 'but if you're not, then ring 0208 687 . . .' Christians must be seekers, pilgrims, explorers, remembering that Christ does not so much answer all our questions as question all our answers.

Several Gospel stories have come to be associated with Mary Magdalene over the years, but we cannot be sure of the accuracy of such claims. What we can know with a fair degree of certainty, for three of the Gospels note it, is that she stood at Calvary, near the foot of the cross. She was the one who was there to the bitter end – she watched and waited as Jesus was tortured and breathed his last. She stood there in all her grief, helpless in the face of his suffering, yet knowing that her being there mattered.

Some time ago now I heard a very poignant interview on the radio. I was driving and found myself pulling over and stopping the car, so intense was the content. A British woman was speaking about her involvement with a prisoner on Death Row. She wrote letters to this man for some years and got to know him very well. He used to say that he wished he could have been part of her family and, if he had, how differently things might have turned out. One day, she received a letter from him, with the request that she had been dreading – asking that she be present on the day of his execution. In fear she agreed to it and went and witnessed something which, of course, changed her life. She saw this man in the flesh – a man whom she'd known only through words on the page of a letter. He was brought in to the chamber of execution, the chaplain stood in front of him, the prison warder behind him. The prisoner looked at each of those gathered and said to his brother, also present, 'I didn't think it would take this much to get you into a suit, brother.' Then he turned to the woman to whom he'd written for years and said, quite simply, 'Thanks for coming all the way with me.'

That was Mary's calling; that is our calling too. Christ asks of us that we walk with him into the dark, frightened and hurting places of his world; he calls us to stand alongside those in whom he is still being crucified today – in the Lebanon, in Afghanistan, Iraq. Our churches are not called to be holy huddles, places of refuge away from the suffering of the world. Rather, we are to be a people who take seriously a crucified God, recognizing in the cries, the struggles, the outrage of those who suffer a God who is strangely present and before whom we, like Mary Magdalene, dare not retreat or close our eyes.

But perhaps Mary Magdalene is best known as being the prime witness at the resurrection. In the narrative of John's Gospel we read of her encounter with the risen Christ in the garden. She mistakes him for the gardener, then realizes her mistake when he speaks her name and goes rushing up to him. He draws back and asks her not to cling to him, but to go. In that little encounter we witness Christ resurrected from the dead, yes, but more than that, we see Mary's potential for resurrection life too. We see her teetering on the brink – desperate to hold on, wanting to preserve life the way it was; needing to make the moment last a little longer. And Christ says, 'No, turn around, go, choose life and tell my friends to do the same.' And in that split second, she is asked to make the choice between death and life; she is asked to opt for resurrection, and invited to follow Christ into an ever open future.

So as we celebrate this most holy saint, may she become for us a dynamic role model as we continue Christ's mission in the world. Like Mary, may we take seriously our calling to be companions of Jesus, travelling with a questing spirit, even when that takes us beyond the familiar and the secure. Like Mary, may we dare to ask and be challenged by the difficult questions for the sake of creating a more just and God-like world. Like Mary, may we be prepared to walk all the way to Calvary, willing to exchange comfort and conformity for the risky, messy business of the gospel. And like Mary may we take leaps of faith, being willing to turn around, letting go of what has gone before with an eagerness to live lives of resurrection in every nook and cranny of God's world.

9 / 11
A reflection on the anniversary

'Come, let us build ourselves a city'

Genesis 11.4

Then they said, 'Come, let us build ourselves a city, and a tower with its top in the heavens, and let us make a name for ourselves; otherwise we shall be scattered abroad upon the face of the whole earth.'

The other evening, having just returned home from New York, my husband was enthusing his family with the photos he took. It was a city he'd always wanted to visit, so having gone there for a conference he took every available opportunity to get out of the confines of the campus, to explore this intoxicating city. Inevitably he had a number of photos of 'Ground Zero'.

The aftershocks of that day rumble dangerously on: the world it seems is constantly on the edge of some imminent apocalyptic atrocity; it seems we live with a social and political fear of upheaval that is further reinforced by the increased turbulence in nature – tsunamis, hurricanes, flooding and bird flu epidemics; indeed, it is a wonder any of us get out of bed in the morning.

The irony is that for all the choice, comfort and apparent control we in the West have over our lives, most of us feel increasingly insecure. Despite the billions of pounds that will be spent this year on anything from bomb-proofing buildings, extra CCTV cameras, home security devices, phone tapping (and now I read we are experimenting with cameras fixed to the heads of police), we actually feel more vulnerable and anxious about the future.

Mike Davies, in his book *Dead Cities* (written in the immediate aftermath of 9/11), reminds his readers that New York has a history of paranoia and anxiety which many noted in the 1920s. He quotes the Spanish poet Federico García Lorca describing a walk he took down Wall Street on the Tuesday in 1929 when the Stock Market collapsed. Lorca watched with stunned amazement as ruined investors flung themselves from the windows of the highest skyscrapers. 'The ambulances collected suicides', he wrote, 'whose hands were full of rings amid the merciless silence of money'; and in that silence, says Davies, Lorca felt the sensation of 'real death, death without hope, death that is nothing but rottenness'.

Meanwhile another Spanish writer, John Dos Passos, wrote a surrealist novel in 1925 called *Manhattan Transfer*. The central character, Jimmy, wanders through Manhattan at night in a kind of waking nightmare – his main fear is that a sky-scraper will fall on top of him (an effect brought on when looking up from street level). Passos writes: 'All these April nights combing the streets alone a skyscraper has obsessed Jimmy – a grooved building jutting up with uncountable bright windows falling into him out of a scudding sky.' Jimmy's other nightmare is that New York feels like an out-of-control steam train, heading for unknown disaster. The sheer velocity of the metropolis, including the drunken swaying of its arrogant skyline, is the master theme of *Manhattan Transfer*. It is not surprising that the passengers on this runaway train should be more than a little anxious.

People jumping out of skyscrapers, collapsing buildings – no wonder Davies sees chilling premonitions of 9/11 in those writing 80 years earlier. For him, cities like New York seem to have acquired their own kinetic energy – an unstoppable urge to self-destruct.

But why? What is the source of this out-of-control death wish?

In seeking the answer to this Davies turns to another pre-war figure, the Marxist writer Ernst Bloch, who in 1929 wrote *The Anxiety of an Engineer*. In it he com-pares two cities, one pre-capitalist, one capitalist. The pre-capitalist example he chooses is Naples, sprawling at the bottom of an active volcano that wiped out the people of Pompeii and Herculaneum. Bloch notes that here there is no delusion of command over nature, just constant adaptation to ecology. Bloch sees Naples as an imperfect, organic city that yields to the fluxes of a dynamic Mediterranean environment where life is allowed to remain in a halfway condition and delight is taken in the way things come to find their own equilibrium. And Bloch observes that, despite facing potential catastrophe more than any other European city, anxiety does not infuse daily life in Naples.

Compare this to the American big city with its quest for a middle-class utopia. Here everything must be locked down and controlled – the city is turned into a totally predictable and safe environment. The highly complex capitalist city spells danger in Bloch's view, because it dominates rather than cooperates with nature. Bloch writes, 'Where technology has achieved an apparent victory over the limits of nature – the more inversely fearful we have become of known and especially unknown danger.' The paradox is that this has led to a profound sense of anxiety and insecurity. Systems that have become so centralized in order to exert control are paradoxically more vulnerable: just one strike will disable the whole social system, be it a hurricane in New Orleans or a plane flying into the financial heart of New York.

And is it not the case that America and other parts of the world are now disabled more by *fear* of violence and destruction than by any actual terrorist event that could be carried out? And might the root of this fear be the overwhelming arrogance and disregard of the human species in believing that it can live as if it were separate and distinct from nature, rather than being at one with its ecology in a balanced equilibrium? Is it not the case that the more we attempt to control the uncontrollable, rather than accept finitude and risk, the more the repressed energy (be it natural or political) will eventually surge over the city barriers we futilely erect?

As I muse on this I am drawn to the story of the Hebrew people, written many, many centuries earlier, whereby they too attempted to build a tower stretching to the heavens, seeing it as a symbol of their strength, self-belief and self-confidence. But that too was short-lived, for Yahweh saw it as another example of sheer human arrogance – a futile human attempt to control and subdue.

So what will now happen to Ground Zero, to that plot of land where the edifices to humanity's insecurity once stood? Might the answer to that question contain within it a kernel of hope for humanity's future? Will that plot of land remain an eloquent testimony to those who died – a space of hubris and quiet reflection? Might it become a park – a place of peacefulness and tranquility?

No, none of that. Instead on 4 July 2006 a 20-tonne cornerstone was laid for 'Freedom Tower', intended to be one of the world's tallest buildings at 541 metres or a third of a mile high. The mayor of New York said that the building expressed the truth that the cause of liberty can never be defeated and that it would stand as a new symbol of American strength and confidence.

No, we have not learnt the lessons, we have not understood.

'Come, let us build ourselves a city, with a tower that reaches to the heavens, so that we might make a name for ourselves'.

Thirst for it

Harvest festival thoughts

Exodus 17.1–7; John 4.4–14

Did you know that a staggering 82 per cent of the world's population recognize the Coca-Cola logo – from the most hi-tech society to the very poorest village community? Some years ago I was fortunate to have a six-month study period in South India and during that time visited many remote rural communities. Many of them had a television placed strategically in the centre of the village for public viewing and the audience, sitting down of an evening to enjoy the latest Bollywood movie, found themselves treated to a consistent diet of Coca-Cola adverts.

Some years ago now Coca-Cola ran a particularly successful advertising campaign with the slogan, 'Thirst for it'. As with all effective ads, the simplicity of the slogan belied a strong and compelling message. It tapped into the universal human experience of being thirsty and so too it spoke of determination, clarity of conviction and the desire to get what you want: the image of an Olympic sprinter determined to win that gold medal comes to mind.

The Hebrew people in today's reading had a deep thirst – probably not for Coca-Cola but for water. There was a water crisis and in a desperate attempt to protect themselves from the glare of the midday sun they each put on their rose-coloured spectacles and looked back the way they had come, deciding they had been better off as slaves back in Egypt. All the evidence they'd accumulated suggested to them that their God had abandoned them and a shortage of water was the final confirmation. 'Is the Lord in our midst or not?' they demanded of Moses. And they had a point, for was it not an ironic cruelty for their leader to be speaking of promised lands flowing with milk and honey while in the meantime their needs could not be met and they were set to die en route? A desperate thirst caused a dramatic change in their behaviour.

And what of us this harvest time? Can a dramatic thirst in us for the earth to be restored to the glory of God motivate us to change our behaviour? All of us know that the harvest we are celebrating is precariously in the balance. Ours is the first generation who cannot say, 'We didn't know.' Every day we open our papers or switch on the television and are alerted to the latest catastrophic figures about global warming, and its effect on the natural world. We know that unless we significantly change our behaviour there may not be a future for our children, let alone our grandchildren.

This festival is a time to celebrate the goodness of the earth and all it yields, to give thanks for those who work so tirelessly to give us food on our tables and to remember before God the cycle of the seasons that enables our fruits to come to maturity. And yet we sit here in some discomfort, knowing that that is only half the story. For we know of the huge disparity between those who enjoy the fruits of the harvest and those who never taste of it. We know that despite impressive campaigns on behalf of fair trading, the majority of those who grow our crops do not receive a fair wage for their labour. In this country evidence is beginning to emerge of a new form of 'bonded labour' where economic migrant workers are being exploited by unscrupulous businesses. We know that one fifth of the world live on less than a dollar a day. We know that one of the eight millennium goals is clean water for all by 2015 and yet a child continues to die every 15 seconds from water-related diseases. And our harvest hymns will ring hollow and haunting this year if we rest on our laurels, kidding ourselves that God is in his heaven and all is right with the world.

So I ask you again, what do you thirst for? Do you share the longing for that vision of the earth that we read about in the opening chapter of our Scriptures – that first creation story depicting an earth in harmony with itself, the seasons, the plants, the animals, all interdependent on one another; humanity at peace with itself, in balance with nature and at one with God? The story's brevity and simplicity has meant that for too long we have confined it to that which we tell our children in their early years – a beautifully crafted tale. Might we now retrieve it and let it act as a catalyst, a deep source of inspiration for us as we seek to build a sustainable future?

What do you thirst for? Jesus spent his life thirsting – thirsting for people to come home to God. In the Gospel reading we have just heard we meet Jesus sweaty and exhausted from a long journey. He sits down by the well at noon when the sun is overhead. There he meets a woman who had come to draw water and in his need he says to her, 'Give me a drink.' And that became the beginning of a remarkable conversation, so remarkable that John notes later in the chapter that the woman was prepared to leave her most treasured possession, her water jar, in order to drink of the living water.

As we celebrate this harvest, may we discover a thirst within ourselves – a thirst that makes us willing to leave behind some of our most treasured possessions, those that get in the way of us acting for a fairer and more humane world. May that thirst translate itself into a deep longing inside us, a longing that makes us, like the Israelites, change our behaviour, so that one day soon the whole of creation might find its thirst quenched and its dignity restored in God.

Celebrating One World

A corporate liturgy for One World Week

The gathering

Leader   O God, you gather us from many places,
              into one community with one another and with you.

All   **We are called to be a people of hospitality**
              living out your life of compassion and healing.

Leader   O God, you gather us from many places,
              into one community and with the whole of creation.

All   **We are called to be a prophetic people**
              living out your life of truth and justice.

              Let us worship the God who makes us one!

Song   **Jesus calls us here to meet him**

              (J. Bell and G. Maule, in *Common Ground: A song book for all the churches*, John L. Bell, Wild Goose Publications, 1994)

              or

              Oh the Earth is the Lord's

              (Psalm 24(23), adapted by Charles Irvine, in John L. Bell, *Common Ground: A song book for all the churches*, Wild Goose Publications, 1994)

Reading *Any of the following would be suitable:*
              Isaiah 58.6–12
              Psalm 24
              Matthew 5.1–10

Reflection

An affirmation of faith

Leader   Creator God, you have breathed life into us,
          not into some of us, but into all of us.

All   **We will live our lives firm in this conviction.**

Leader   Creator God, you have stamped your divine image on our hearts,
          not on some of us, but on all of us.

All   **We will live our lives firm in this knowledge.**

Leader   Creator God, you urge us to claim our full dignity in you,
          not just some of us, but all of us.

All   **We will live our lives firm in this assurance.**

Leader   Creator God, you love the world so much that you go on giving in love,
          not to some of us, but to all of us.

All   **We will live our lives firm in this belief.**

Leader   Creator God,
          give us the wisdom to discern
          and the determination to walk the path
          that leads to peace.

Prayers may be offered focusing upon contemporary events. Each prayer may finish with the following response:

Leader   Save us from being overwhelmed

All   **but deliver us from a comfortable conscience.**

Song   **Alleluia! Raise the gospel**

        (Bernadette Farrell, *Go Before Us*, OCP Publications, 2003)

        or

        If you believe and I believe

        (*Hymns Old and New: One church, one faith, one Lord*, Kevin Mayhew, 2004

Closing responses of commitment

Leader   Stretch out your hand!
All   **So we may learn the art of being
God's healing touch in the world.**

Leader   Position your feet!
All   **So we might be better placed to walk
God's wounded steps in the world.**

Leader   Sense your heartbeat!
All   **So our souls might expand and become
God's generous hospitality in the world.**

Leader   Open your eyes!
All   **So our focus might sharpen and we see
God's image reflected in all who inhabit this world.**

Standing on holy ground

A retreat to consider our relationship with the earth

Various focus points, representing the different days of creation, are set out in different parts of the room. There will need to be adequate space between each point, so that one does not impose upon another, and each stands in its own right.

The leader slowly and sensitively guides the participants through the following exercise (or one of her/his choosing):

Find a suitable place to lie down. (If this is not appropriate then participants are invited to sit comfortably in a chair with both feet placed firmly on the ground.)
Be aware of your breathing. Breathe in deeply and feel the breath entering your lungs.
Relax your muscles and the whole of your body.
Be aware of the earth beneath you and your connection with it.
Sense yourself held and strengthened by the earth.
Continue to focus on your breathing. Breathe in deeply and as you breathe out let go of all tension, all anxiety.
Be at peace with the earth.

When you are ready, in your own time, take your seat in the room.

Introductions

Invite participants to introduce themselves to one another, and ask them to say why they have come, and what is their particular curiosity/concern that is alive within them at present.

It is important that adequate time is given to introductions.

Reading

Genesis 1.1—2.3 is read aloud.

Participants are invited to share their reaction to the reading. How familiar was the story? Was there anything they felt they were hearing for the first time? Was there anything that struck a chord with them or, conversely, something that they felt discomfort with?

Note the darkness that enveloped everything before time began, then note the order out of chaos, the carefully structured universe where everything has its place; not a strong sense of interconnectedness but the whole taken together is 'complete'.

Matthew Fox, theologian, in *A New Reformation: Creation spirituality and the transformation of Christianity*, Inner Traditions, 2006, has this to say: 'The dark night of the soul is a learning place of great depth. Stillness is required. Not only is there a dark night of the soul, but also a dark night of society and a dark night of our species.' So have we come full circle? Is there a sense, in our time, that once again there is 'darkness over the deep' with the impending ecological catastrophe, while God's spirit hovers, waiting for a new order to be born? Can we give birth to it before it is too late?

Participants are invited to discuss these questions.

Focus points

Participants are then invited to move around the various 'focus points' highlighting the 'seven days' of creation, spending time responding to each as appropriate.

Day 1 Light and dark, day and night

'Let there be light'

Paint, brushes, water, fabric, seeds, stones and other natural pieces appropriate for a collage should be laid out on a table and a long length of plain wallpaper is rolled out.

Participants are invited to add their contribution to a collage, illustrating order and chaos, light and dark.

Day 2 Heaven and earth

'Praise him, you highest heavens'

A display board with photographs of places of pilgrimage around the world forms the focal point. Cushions are placed for people to sit on and meditate.

George MacLeod described the tiny Scottish island of Iona as a 'thin place', where only a tissue paper separated the material from the spiritual.

Participants are invited to think of examples from their own experience that speak to them of a strong sense of place, where heaven and earth are intimately connected. Why is that so? What is their association with that place? What does it tell them about their relationship with the earth?

Day 3 Earth, seas and vegetation

'. . . plants bearing seed in their several kinds'

Facts and figures are presented, especially about global warming, migration of people, plundering of resources.

At this focus point people can read facts and figures about global warming, migration of people across the globe and the plundering of the natural world. In the middle of these facts there is the beginning of a liturgy of penitence that reads:

God says, 'Take off your shoes, for you stand on holy ground.'
Is it still holy, Lord,
When we have re-coursed the rivers to pander to our needs?
When we have pushed living creatures to the edge of extinction?
When we have poisoned the air with our ever cheaper air flights?
When we have . . .

Participants are invited to add their own words to this liturgy.

Day 4 Galaxy, sun and moon

'The vault of heaven to shine on the earth'

At this focus point there is a selection of sacred texts from the major world religions, including the Bible, which is open at Psalm 148.

Paper and pens are available and participants are invited to write a psalm in praise of creation, considering both the fragility and the strength of the universe that connects the web of life.

Day 5 Sea creatures and birds

'. . . every type of living creatures with which the waters teem'

At this focus point there is a graffiti board and a pen. It is surrounded by newspaper cuttings, statements of fact, and appropriate quotations concerning the pollution of the oceans.

Participants are invited to add their own statement to the graffiti board.

Day 6 Wild beasts, land creatures and human beings

'male and female, he created them in his image'

At this focus point there is a large globe.

Participants are invited to write a statement of belief emphasizing (a) their understanding of humanity's relationship with the rest of creation and (b) their understanding of humanity created in God's beauty and image.

Day 7 Resting and blessing

Creation is complete and God draws breath.

Participants are invited either to spend time in silent meditation/prayer or to go outside and be attentive to all the sounds that are around them.

(If the retreat is being run over a weekend, it would be appropriate to go on a **pilgrimage walk**. Here the facilitator would be familiar with the walk and offer appropriate prayers en route.)

Closing liturgy

This incorporates the work of the day or weekend and includes a sharing of bread and wine.

Participants are seated in a circle, with the contributions from the focus points placed in the middle of the room.

Opening statement

We know that the whole creation has been groaning in labour pains until now; and not only the creation, but we ourselves, who have the first fruits of the Spirit, grown inwardly while we wait for adoption, the redemption of our bodies.

Romans 8.22–23

In praise of creation

- A song or chant in celebration of creation may be sung
- Psalms written by participants are read aloud (Day 4)

And yet . . .

Litany of repentance

- Words and statements from the graffiti board are called out at random (Day 5)
- The Confessional statement is read out by various participants. Each statement may be interspersed with a chant of penitence (Day 3)

The goodness of the earth

- Stories are shared reflecting that holy 'sense of place' (Day 2)
- Bread and wine are shared one with another, possibly introduced with the following words:

  Through God's goodness we have this bread to share, which earth has given and human hands have made.
  Through God's goodness we have this wine to share, fruit of the vine, and work of human hands.
  Through God's goodness we have ourselves to offer, fruit of the womb and created in God's image.

Commitment to the task ahead

- After the sharing of the bread and wine all commit themselves to being co-creators with God as each person reads our their statement of belief (Day 6)

God's blessing as we journey on

- The following words based on an ancient Celtic blessing are offered (or danced if appropriate):

  Deep peace of the running wave to you,
  Deep peace of the flowing air to you,
  Deep peace of the quiet earth to you,
  Deep peace of the shining stars to you,
  Deep peace of the Son of Peace to you.

Encircling love

Questions and exercises to explore All Hallows' Eve

The origins of Hallowe'en can be traced back to the Celtic tribes. They celebrated the start of the New Year and the coming of Winter on 1 November. The night before was the Festival of Samhain, Lord of the Dead, and was the time the spirits of the deceased roamed the earth, having one last throw of the die before the new year set in. But it was not just the good spirits that made their presence known – so too the evil ones intermingled with the living and, in an effort to ward them off, people would cover their faces with ghoulish masks and light fires.

In the ninth century Pope Gregory IV deliberately moved the celebration of All Saints from its date in May to that of 1 November. In a conscious effort to Christianize the Celtic festivals, the emphasis moved from celebrating the new year to celebrating those exemplars of the Christian faith who had died – the 'hallowed' or 'holy ones'. Thus the night before became the vigil: All Hallows' Eve.

A couple of centuries later, an influential abbot encouraged the extension of the feast of All Saints and chose 2 November to be the day when the Church remembered all who had died, not simply the 'saintly'.

So in a sense Hallowe'en is a vigil for both these celebrations, for All Saints and for All Souls.

Here are some questions and exercises to encourage an exploration of this season:

- What are your own memories of Hallowe'en?
- In medieval times many believed that if you had not been reconciled to someone before their death, then their spirit would return to taunt you. As a result many people would offer 'treats' to the spirit of the deceased on All Hallows' Eve. Is there something here around the Christian concept of forgiveness that might be salvaged and transformed?
- Do you have a strong sense of an afterlife? If so, how might you define it?
- The following prayer from the Celtic tradition calls upon the power of the natural elements to protect the people from evil. The Christian tradition has for much of its history operated with a theology of humanity's dominance over nature, contributing to the present ecological crisis of our planet. How do you understand a spirituality that seeks to work in harmony with nature? Where is it being expressed?

At Tara today in this fateful hour
I place all heaven with its power,
And the sun with its brightness,
And the snow with its whiteness,
And the fire with all the strength it hath,
And the lightning with its rapid wrath,
And the winds with their swiftness along the path,
And the sea with its deepness,
And the earth with its starkness:
All these I place
By God's almighty grace,
Between myself and the powers of darkness.

Attributed to St Patrick, from *The Edge of Glory: Prayers in the Celtic tradition*, by David Adam, Triangle/SPCK, 1985

- The Celts also performed a ritual to express their profound belief in the presence of God all around them and within them. Known as the Caim, the ritual was performed in a number of ways but in its essence it was the creation of a sacred circle around that which needed God's protection. Here was no magic, but rather the calling to mind of a deep-seated sense of God's presence in, and upholding of, all creation. A person might stand with their right arm stretched out and the index finger extended, then turn, toward the sun, walking slowly full circle with outstretched arm, calling on the presence, and chanting a prayer.

  What is the place of such rituals in a contemporary expression of faith? Consider writing your own prayer, calling on God's protection to encircle you.

A final prayer

Keep at bay, dear God,
all that holds the potential to harm me.
Keep at arm's length
the spirit of malice and deceit,
the spirit of hypocrisy and petty-mindedness,
the spirit of self-deception and false humility.
Expand your spirit within my soul
that I may move from fear to trust,
and in so doing
sense the aura of your life and love
encircling me in its light.
Amen

Part Four

A Place at the Table
Journeying toward Christmas

To thee I give...

A strange sort of homecoming

Thoughts inspired by Mark 6.1–6

Mark 6.1–6

He left that place and came to his home town, and his disciples followed him. On the sabbath he began to teach in the synagogue, and many who heard him were astounded. They said, 'Where did this man get all this? What is this wisdom that has been given to him? What deeds of power are being done by his hands! Is not this the carpenter, the son of Mary and brother of James and Joses and Judas and Simon, and are not his sisters here with us?' And they took offence at him. Then Jesus said to them, 'Prophets are not without honour, except in their home town, and among their own kin, and in their own house.' And he could do no deed of power there, except that he laid his hands on a few sick people and cured them. And he was amazed at their unbelief.

A strange sort of homecoming for Jesus, wasn't it? The place where he might have expected to have been welcomed with open arms, clasped into the bosom of his family, became instead a breeding ground for hostility and resentment. The hostility seemed to stem from those who 'knew how a carpenter's son should act' . . . 'and it isn't like this'. Jesus had brought embarrassment on his own community, resulting in deep rejection. Look a bit more closely at the text, and you might be left wondering what his immediate family made of it all; were they a part of those who, we are told, 'did not accept him', or might Mary have been observing at a distance, as she had so many times before, holding in her heart all that she saw, turning it over in her mind with the wisdom of a mother?

But what was Jesus expecting? Was he not being a bit naive? After all, they say you can never return to a place you once left – both you and it will have changed and you cannot reclaim what is no longer there. I recall last year running a retreat for a group of 15 people. They had come to the Retreat House from different parts of the country and were there to explore the concept of the extravagant love of God. At the beginning of one session I placed a series of black and white sketches on the floor, each depicting some aspect of 'homecoming'; the participants were invited to pick up the one they felt most drawn to, the one with which they felt most affinity. As people spoke of the picture they had chosen, the evident pain of 'home-coming' was clear for all to see. One woman spoke of a return home as a young adult, only to discover her parents had split up and her mother's new partner had placed his feet firmly under the table; another spoke of home as a place to escape from, due to the deceit and abusive relationships that had characterized his upbringing. And yet another spoke of her constant search for a place of acceptance, that might be defined as a 'coming home', but which to date had eluded her.

Our Scriptures speak a great deal about homecoming – the theme weaves in and out of the biblical narrative. It is linked of course to that of exile, the Hebrew people's bondage to foreign powers and alien rule that characterized various stages of their history. Some of the most poignant and heartfelt writings of our Scriptures come from these times, when the people longed for a return home, both in a physical sense and so, too, a yearning for their souls to be at one with their God. And whenever they lost that desire, whenever they sat contentedly amid an alien power, the prophets attempted to call them back, back to the God of their ancestors and to the heart of their God.

And that same biblical theme continues today – exile, alienation and rootlessness characterize the lives of so many people. The number of those migrating across the globe grows daily; the number of people who find themselves in a place of exile, a stranger in a strange land, increases day by day. And as the scarce resources of the world continue to be plundered and grabbed by the few, so the numbers of displaced people is set to rise. Amnesty International tells us that the abuse of human rights around the world is worse now than it has ever been, that an increasing number of people live with the reality or fear of persecution, torture, physical and mental abuse. And every day people are arriving at our ports and the moment they arrive they find themselves to be 'non'-people, people without status, resulting in mental and physical insecurity.

Yet such people as these continue to hold within themselves a deep desire for home. The refugees and asylum seekers with whom I worked as a minister in Milton Keynes had heart-rending stories to tell of the dislocation that they experienced in an alien culture, where they found little with which to identify and even less to feel at home in. Each year Scargill welcomes a group of asylum seekers over the threshold to see in the New Year and often the prayer uppermost on their lips is their desire to return home, to a place that will offer them a sense of community and homecoming.

All of us need to discover a sense of home. As I read this story of Jesus' sense of separation from home, I can't help but wonder whether it stands as a defining moment in his ministry. Following this encounter did he always find himself on the edge, at odds with those with whom he'd spent so much of his life? And did he realize, at that moment, the need to discover a sense of home elsewhere? As I read the Gospels, I have a hunch that it was in the company of Mary and Martha that

Jesus might have experienced that sense of homecoming. Perhaps there, in the company of good friends, he could be himself, share the frustrations and joys of the day, chew over the gossip of the village, put his feet up and let his hair down over a good meal.

Homecoming will of course take a different shape for each of us for our restlessness takes different forms, we fear different things, and our inner exiles form a part of our own unique story. In the novel, *The Sea*, by John Banville (Picador, 2005), the main character, Max Morden, poignantly expresses that yearning to come home to oneself, to be at peace in the universe. As Max struggles to come to terms with the loss and grief of losing his wife through cancer, he muses on his life:

> When I look back I see that the greater part of my energies was always given over to the simple search for shelter, for comfort, for, yes, I admit it, for cosiness. This is a surprising, not to say a shocking, realisation. Before, I saw myself as something of a buccaneer, facing all-comers with a cutlass in my teeth, but now I am compelled to acknowledge that this was a delusion. To be concealed, protected, guarded, that is all I have ever truly wanted, to burrow down into a place of womby warmth and cower there, hidden from the sky's indifferent gaze and the harsh air's damagings.

And perhaps the challenge for the Church, at a time when there is so much fragmentation going on both around us and within us, is to be a place of homecoming. Can the Church live up to its calling to incarnate a God whose ultimate desire is for each of us to find a home in his love? Can our churches learn to be places of true homecoming for those who feel a sense of alienation, dislocation, or inner exile? Too many people look on at the Church from a distance, in benign amusement, boredom or disbelief at the way in which it occupies its time at present. Debates in the Anglican Church over the place of gay people, over the authority of women in the hierarchy of the Church, and over definitive statements of belief around which people are asked to unite continue to be high on its agenda. Is it too naive to hope that, one day soon, the Church will move beyond its present preoccupation with who is in and who is out, which only adds to a deep sense of exile for some?

St Augustine, way back in the third century, wrote, 'Our hearts are restless till they find their rest in Thee.' To know ourselves held in the ultimate embrace of God is to be at peace within ourselves and with the world around us. May we discover the reality of that for ourselves this Advent and may we in turn be bearers of that truth to those who are yearning for home.

Waiting on God in an uncertain world:
The prayer of protest and passion

A biblical reflection
(appropriate for a full or half day retreat)

Waiting implies passivity; however, taking some of the more flamboyant biblical characters, we ask how their own prayers of passion and protest might inspire and influence our own waiting on God in an uncertain world.

You will need

- magazines/newspapers
- candles and matches
- pens and paper
- CD player and CDs (see suggestion for music)

Introduction: The prayer of lament

This has been defined as the 'way you respond when faith and experience collide painfully with one another' (Gordon Mursell, *Praying in Exile*, DLT, 2005, p. 40).
  Many of the psalms illustrate this with questions such as:

- Why did you allow this to happen, God?
- Why is this happening to me?
- What have we done to you, Yahweh, to provoke this response in you?

Many psalms challenge God to do something. The psalmists wrestle with God in order to make sense of the pain and injustice of the world or of their particular situation.

Read extracts from psalms that express this, e.g. Psalms 10, 13, 77

The importance of these psalms of lament within the Judaeo/Christian tradition is perhaps threefold:

98

- Theological: the chaos of the world, against which so many of the psalms rail, is seen as a reversal of the process of bringing order out of chaos that marked the Hebrew understanding of the way God acts in the world (see the creation myth of Genesis 1). The frequent use of the image of drowning would seem to underline this. For examples, see Psalms 69.1–2, 88.7–8.
- Psychological: the depth and authenticity of the people's relationship with Yahweh was the groundrock upon which they would stand to hurl their anger, shock and bemusement at Yahweh. It was precisely because they had tasted of his unconditional love that they had courage and honesty in confronting their God. For an example of this see Psalm 10.1.
- Holistic: these psalms are concerned with the whole of life. They bring together both the personal and the political; no part of life was considered to be beyond the responsibility or interest of Yahweh. For an example of this see Psalm 102.

Each participant is given a psalm of lament to read while traditional and/or contemporary musical settings of the psalms are played

Where do the sentiments expressed in these psalms resonate with you?
What do you/would you protest about? How do you/would you express it?

Job

Tell the story of Job in your own way, emphasizing the following:

- Job's friends represent a 'top-down' approach to theology, where faith begins with external doctrinal principles which are then rigidly applied to human experience. Job represents the opposite – a 'bottom-up' approach, whereby his faith expressed through prayer is a direct articulation of his experience.
- Job protests against his own unjust situation and moves from there to a protest on behalf of suffering humanity (see Job 24.12). He confronts the dilemma for all people of faith, namely, why does God allow suffering of the innocent?
- In the end God answers Job, but the 'end' is a long time coming. Much of the book is characterized by God's seeming absence.

Participants consider the following:

Have there been times in your life when you have hurled your questions into the darkness, when the absence, rather than the presence, of God has seemed more of a reality?

Jonah

Tell the story of Jonah in your own way (or read the Old Testament narrative), emphasizing the following:

- Anger, impulsiveness and sulkiness characterize much of Jonah's prayer before Yahweh.
- In this story the Hebrew people's capacity for humour and irony is clearly seen (not least in Yahweh's teasing of Jonah with the castor oil plant) and reflects something of their approach to God.

Participants consider the following:

What aspects of the story resonate with your experience of God? Does Jonah's childish response to Yahweh echo an aspect of your own relationship with God?

What part does humour play in your relationship with God?

Moses

Read the story of the creation of the golden calf found in Exodus 32. Then empha-size the following:

- The story contrasts two, very different, prayers of protest. One is represented by the Israelite people whose anger at Yahweh over their situation results in their rejecting him and replacing him with an idol that they could manage and be in control over. The other prayer is articulated by Moses; he represents the prayer of waiting and silence followed by vehement anger, argument and challenge of Yahweh's wisdom.
- God is presented here (in his argument with Moses) not as some distant, change-less dispenser of fate, but rather as an adversary, a friend, one who will enter into a relationship and be prepared to be changed by it.

Participants consider the following:

Is God someone with whom you can push your questions hard, whom you can challenge and to whom you can protest? Where have you opted for a 'golden calf' instead – a malleable substitute, a mascot, whom you can control?

Write a contemporary psalm that reflects your own prayer of lament.

Is there another biblical character or contemporary figure who has given you an insight into what the prayer of protest and passion might look like?

Closing liturgy

Songs of protest from the world Church are played as background music throughout the liturgy, with the volume raised between sections of the liturgy.
Appropriate music can be found on the following CDs:

> Many and Great: World Church songs *(vol. 1), John L. Bell and Graham Maule, Wild Goose Publications, 1990*
> Psalms of Patience, Protest and Praise: 23 psalm settings, *John L. Bell, Wild Goose Publications, 1993*

Participants are invited to look through newspapers/magazines and tear out articles or pictures that might provide a focal point for prayer in keeping with the theme of the day. These are placed in the centre of the circle

Psalm 77 (or another) is read, with each participant reading a verse aloud

As the music continues participants are invited to place a lit candle on one of the newspaper cuttings and read aloud their own prayer of protest, formulated during the day

The liturgy concludes with the following affirmation of faith:

Leader	In an uncertain world,
All	**We will wait on God**
	And not fear the shifting sands.
Leader	In a complex and confusing world,
All	**We will wait on God**
	and live with the contradictions.
Leader	In a world that seeks the answers,
All	**We will wait on God**
	And dare to live the questions.
Leader	In an uncertain world,
All	**We will wait on God.**

I am indebted to the writings of Gordon Mursell in *Out of the Deep* (DLT, 1989) and *Praying in Exile* (DLT, 2005) for inspiration for this chapter.

The riches of darkness

Advent thoughts

My second child was born a few days before Christmas; inevitably, with Christmas being uppermost in everyone's minds, he and I missed out on the flood of cards that tend to accompany a birth. But I remember a Christmas card that year that made me both chuckle and cry as I struggled to feed my Christmas bundle in the depths of the night. The card held the picture of a dishevelled Mary, slumped in an arm-chair, every bone of her body oozing exhaustion, feet in a bowl of hot water, mug of hot chocolate in one hand and baby, screaming with nappy half off, in the other arm. And the aloof cat was stretched out on the arm of the chair, with one ear on proceedings, yet keeping a respectable distance. The caption at the bottom of the Christmas card read, quite simply, 'After the birth'.

I warmed to the card, not simply because of its obvious affinity with my situation but because it didn't pull any punches. No place here for saccharine babies, asleep and at peace in their mothers' arms, no place here for the contented Madonna with not a hair out of place. Here, the mess and the dark side of childbirth were all intermingled with the wonder of the new life.

We've now entered the season of Advent and you might say the countdown to Christmas has begun. Traditionally, it was of course less to do with a counting down the days and much more to do with getting your house in order (a sort of mini Lent) so that your own life, and that of the Church, might be a fitting place for God to come to birth once more. Yet while the Church still offers something of that in its liturgy, there's much less credence paid to that discipline. It's as though we want to romp quickly through all that in order to arrive at the joy and light of Christmas Day. It's as though we want to grasp all the Christmas goodies without having had a hand in their preparation.

Sometimes I wonder whether our Advent hymns are a bit guilty of encouraging all of this. Do some of the finest hymns of this season actually let us off the hook a bit? They call us on to Christmas, encouraging us to strain toward the light, and yet are less committed to encouraging us to stand in the pre-Christmas darkness, that time of waiting, that period of gestation, of wondering, pondering, hoping and fearing.

O Come, thou Dayspring, come and cheer
Our spirits by thine Advent here.
Disperse the gloomy clouds of night,
And death's dark shadows put to flight.

Are we being encouraged to shun the darkness as quickly as possible?

No doubt there is much darkness in our lives that we would want to shun. I know that for myself there is the darkness of fear – fear that what I am is not good enough, that who I am does not match what is required. Then there's the darkness of my belief, a sense that however much I yearn to embrace the gospel message with the whole of my being, there is nevertheless always that part of me that holds back, that refuses to put all my eggs in one basket. And then there is the darkness I create for myself when I turn away from my sisters and brothers and pretend that the desires of the poorest were never meant to be satisfied.

Yet that is not the whole picture. The life of the one whose coming we prepare for during Advent was a full testament to the darkness and suffering that a human being can endure. The road to Bethlehem to which we look forward winds its way past the stable, up to the place of the skull and the day when the sky darkened and the temple curtain was torn in two. Far from fleeing the darkness, the God whose coming we await entered right into the very heart of it.

And so too did the prophet Isaiah. He encouraged people to enter that dark place. Indeed, he spoke of it as being the context out of which a relationship with God might emerge. 'I will give you the treasures of darkness . . . so that you may know that it is I, the Lord, the God of Israel, who call you by your name' (Isaiah 45.3). And surely our own understanding of the world and our experience of it would tend to underline Isaiah's belief that the darkness is a breeding ground for creativity. Consider our children who are conceived in the darkness of their mother's womb, stars that are born in the darkness of space, images and ideas created in the darkness of the brain, the seed preparing for growth in the darkness of the soil; far from being something from which we should flee, the darkness, if we allow it, may become the breeding ground for God's creativity and life to come to birth in us.

My own experience of living in communities has taught me that so much of my time is spent in avoiding that dark space. It is all too easy to hold up the busyness of my life as a smokescreen, shielding me from authentic reflection. At times even the corporate prayer that I value so highly becomes another barrier, with beautifully crafted words and phrases skimming me across the surface of encounter with God, as though their task were, at all costs, to stop me falling into that deep abyss, that dark unfathomable place where God's presence might be found. As John O'Donohue says in his classic book *Anam Cara*, 'The eternal comes to us mainly in terms of nothingness and emptiness. Where there is no space, the eternal cannot visit. Where there is no space, the soul cannot awaken.'

In the end I know that I cannot have the light without the darkness, I cannot have the definition without the shadow, I cannot have the birth without the death. Such paradoxes are woven into the balance of the universe, woven into the Christian story and seen ultimately, for those who follow Christ, in the crucifixion/resurrection paradox.

So perhaps we need to take with a slight pinch of salt those festive cards soon to be dropped through our letter boxes, which obliterate any hint of the dark side of life, the murkiness and messiness that make up our existence. Perhaps we need to adopt a tongue-in-cheek attitude to some of those ancient hymns that encourage us to shun the darkness and step effortlessly into the light. If we do that, perhaps then we can begin to enter more fully into Advent, tentatively welcoming the opportunity it offers us, not for escapism, but for realism, knowing that in the end both the darkness and the light are held within the heartbeat of God.

Prayers for the Advent season

Amid all that gives the lie to God,
surprise us, Jesus, with your birth,
empower us with your presence.
Amid all that tramples dead our dreams,
surprise us, Jesus, with your birth,
empower us with your presence.
Amid all that contradicts your love,
surprise us, Jesus, with your birth,
empower us with your presence,
that finally, free from all our fears,
we may revel in your incarnation.

When the journey is made in the dark
and the terrain is unfamiliar;
when the end is a long way off
and the outcome cannot be predicted;
when the original dream has all but died
for every door has been slammed shut –
then,
stripped of all my defences,
let me feel the birthpangs,
and the force of your life
straining to be born in me.

God of exiles, keep calling us home.
You know how easily we can lose our way –
    our false starts and our stumblings in the dark.
Yet your heartbeat feels the yearnings of our souls;
    you sense our desire for authentic living.
May this Advent season be a time of coming home
    to the very best of who we are.

When my spirit grows faint

Corporate prayer for those who suffer

Leader   When my spirit grows faint within me,
All   **it is you who knows my way.**   *Psalm 142.3*

Voice 1   For all whose bodies frustrate them,
           who struggle with ill health;
           for all awaiting a diagnosis,
           for those preparing for death, we pray . . .

In silence or aloud, we remember those who need our prayers

Leader   When my spirit grows faint within me,
All   **it is you who know my way.**

Voice 2   For all who live in fear:
           fear of violence, fear of abuse;
           for all who live the pain of addiction and who yearn to be free;
           and for those who cannot forgive themselves, we pray . . .

In silence or aloud, we remember those who need our prayers

Leader   When my spirit grows faint within me
All   **it is you who know my way.**

Voice 3   For all who are far from home:
           for asylum seekers and refugees,
           for those held in detention centres,
           and for those who live out their lives behind prison bars, we pray . . .

In silence or aloud, we remember those who need our prayers

Leader   When my spirit grows faint within me,
All   **it is you who know my way.**

Voice 4   For all who are gathered here in prayer,
          and especially for ourselves –
          for the fears and resentments we harbour inside,
          and for all that rises to trouble us, we pray . . .

In silence we pray for ourselves

Leader   When my spirit grows faint within me
All   **it is you who know my way.**

And yet . . .

A confession for the season of Advent

As we take stock of our lives in preparation for the coming of Christ, so we recognize the inherent contradictions in our discipleship:

Advent God,
in this sacred space
and in this expectant time,
we face together that which we may not dare to confront alone:
that our hearts yearn for your love,
yet can be cold toward others;
that our voices sing your praise,
yet so often put others down;
that our feet are asked to walk your steps,
yet prefer to side-step your hurting world;
that our hands are asked to be open to you,
yet become clenched through fear and mistrust;
that our very selves, created in your beauty and image,
refuse to receive your love.

Pause

Let us now claim the freedom of life that God offers us this day:

**We accept God's forgiveness for ourselves
and offer it to the world.
We are loved by God this day, every day,
and for all eternity,
Amen**

Taking our leave

Prayers for the ending of worship

Words in bold are to be said by all

The hills and the dales speak of your glory from one generation to another.
O Lord, our Lord, how majestic is your name in all the earth.

As we prepare to leave this sacred space, let us bring to mind those whom we have encountered this week – both the familiar faces and the new.

Silence

Let us recall the chance conversations and the deliberate sharing of lives.

Silence

Let us bring to mind the moments that have reawakened new life within us.

Silence

Let us prepare ourselves for all that awaits us as we journey on.

Silence

And in our departing let us pray for God's blessing and God's peace to be ours.

Silence

The hills and the dales speak of your glory from one generation to another.
O Lord, our Lord, how majestic is your name in all the earth.

Christ our Companion,
we go on our way
confident of your presence alongside us.
Wherever life takes us,
we will depend on you.
Whatever life demands of us,
we will place faith in you.
Whenever life feels more like death,
we will break through with you.
In you we live, today and for ever,
Amen

Human Rights Day
10 December

An affirmation of faith

Leader   In a death-dealing world
All   We will not give up on life
Leader   In a tired and hurting world
All   We will not give up on life
Leader   In a divided and suspicious world
All   We will not give up on life

Leader   When so many are denied so much
All   We will search for signs of hope
Leader   When so many live with fear
All   We will search for signs of hope
Leader   When so many settle for half-truths
All   We will search for signs of hope

Leader   And should our spirit fail us
All   We will trust the risen One
Leader   And should our flame be dampened down
All   We will trust the risen One
Leader   And should life's knocks cause us to fall
All   We will trust the risen One

Leader   In a death-dealing world
All   We will not give up on life

Giving birth to God

A retreat for mothers with young(ish) children

Aim: to explore the connections between early experiences of mothering and an incarnational God.

Note: It is important to consider running a crèche or offering childcare in order to enable mothers with young children to participate.

The leader may find the following book a good resource in preparing the retreat: Margaret Hebblethwaite, *Motherhood and God*, Geoffrey Chapman, new edition 1993.

You will need

- modelling clay and boards for each individual to work on
- paint and/or pastels
- pens
- paper of varying sizes
- glue
- resources from the natural world, such as: grains, seeds, leaves, feathers, wool, bark (unless the retreat is happening in a place where participants can easily gather their own)

Introduction

The retreat leader shares how the day will run and gives any 'ground rules' for the day, e.g. issues around confidentiality, sensitivity and the uniqueness of every participant's experience.

Relaxation exercise

The leader slowly and sensitively guides the participants through the following exercise (or one of her own choosing):

Sit comfortably with your feet placed firmly on the ground.
Focus on your breathing. Be aware of the breath entering your lungs.
Breathe out slowly.
Beginning at the crown of your head, be aware of each part of your body in turn.
As you move through your body, tense the muscles and hold the tension.
Then relax and, as you do so, breathe out slowly.
Allow the relaxation to enter your mind.
Relinquish each thought that enters your head.
Allow the pool to become still.

When everyone has had adequate time to 'unwind', participants are invited to introduce themselves, speak about their children and why they chose to participate in the day. (They may have been asked in advance to bring photographs of their children to share at this point.)

Preparations for childbirth

Participants are invited to share their experiences as facilitated by the leader.

Luke 1.26–45 is read aloud

We can only imagine Mary's pregnancy experiences. We are told she 'found favour with God' yet the text offers us too little of the human Mary. Perhaps there is a passivity in the way she is presented that is frustrating for us, or perhaps by contrast we can relate to the one who takes it all in and muses on the inevitability of what will take place.

- What might it mean to prepare a home in which God might be nurtured in your life?
- Since having your child/children, how has your own understanding of God and your experience of God changed and developed?

Labour

Participants are invited to share their experiences as facilitated by the leader.

Luke 2.1–20 is read aloud

The shepherds were offered a glorious fanfare of angels announcing the birth of Jesus, but the 'sign' they were given, that of a newborn baby in a cattle shed, could easily have been overlooked or misidentified.

- How do you relate to this paradox? Are you more in sympathy with one aspect than the other? Have you known a fanfare of angels in your own experience, where God's presence has been overwhelming and indisputable, or is God more 'incognito' in your life?
- How would you know when something 'of God' is coming to birth in you?

Crossing the threshold – becoming a parent

The leader may choose to introduce this part of the day through sharing something of her own early experiences of parenting, or simply introducing some of the possible themes to explore, e.g. self-identity, inner resources for mothering, dark times and unexpected joy, changing relationships.

Participants are then asked to hold silence together as they reflect on their own experience of both being mothered and of mothering. When they have had time to consider this they are invited to express, through creative art, an aspect of motherhood that has been/is important for them. They may choose to work with clay, pastels, paint, items from the natural world such as seeds, leaves, stones. For any who prefer not to work in this way, an alternative might be to write a poem or a psalm expressing something of their own experience of motherhood.

Sharing of the day and blessing as we leave

With everyone seated in a circle, the central focus is the collection of creative pieces produced earlier in the day by the participants. A central candle is lit

Leader   Advent God,
             the paradox is:
             you who brought us to birth
             yearn to be born in us.

Song   **Everyday God**

             (Bernadette Farrell, *Restless Is the Heart*, OCP Publications, 2000)

Each participant is invited to share her creative piece. At the end of each contribution a member of the group lights a candle from the central one and offers the following words:

    May God who brought you to birth
    be born in you once more.

At the end of the sharing each participant raises her lit candle as the leader says:

So receive a blessing for all that is demanded of you.
Be a blessing to all who demand from you.
Live the blessing that God has been and will be to you,
this Advent and way beyond,
Amen

Part Five

Seasonal Recipes from Scargill

Part Five

Selected Essays from Kemball

To warm the heart

Favourite recipes

Carrot and coriander roulade   serves 5

1 medium-sized onion
225g / 8 oz grated carrot
25g / 1 oz butter
2 Tbsp chopped parsley
50g / 2 oz wholemeal flour
salt and pepper
1 tsp ground coriander
220g / 8 oz soft cream cheese (or according to taste)
fresh coriander
4 medium-sized eggs

Grease and line a swiss-roll tin or tray.

Finely chop the onion. Melt the butter in a saucepan and sauté the onion till transparent then add grated carrot and ground coriander. Sauté for a minute or two then take off the heat. Add chopped parsley and season generously with salt and pepper. Pour mixture on to a clean chopping board and allow to cool.

Whisk eggs and a pinch of salt in a bowl until thick and creamy (until the trail of the whisk stays in the mixture). Chop the cooled onion and carrot a little then add the carrot mixture and flour to the eggs and fold in carefully. Pour the mixture on to the tray and level it out. Bake in the oven at 200°C / 400°F / gas mark 6 for 10–12 minutes until even and firm to the touch.

Turn out on to a piece of greaseproof paper and roll the mix, keeping the paper in between the roulade. Leave to cool on a wire tray. While cooling, mix the cream cheese and fresh coriander together. Then carefully unroll the roulade and spread on the cheese mixture. Re-roll and serve hot.

Meat loaf and peppercorn sauce   serves 4–6

500g / 1 lb minced beef
1 large onion
1 large red pepper
1 tsp basil
1 medium-sized egg
salt and pepper

Dice onion and pepper and place in a bowl with the mince, basil and egg. Season well and mix together thoroughly. Remove from the bowl and mould into a loaf shape.

Take a piece each of parchment and tin foil big enough to wrap the loaf. Place the parchment on the tin foil, then place the meat loaf on the parchment and wrap like a purse so that the juices are kept in. Put on a tray and place in the oven at 180°C / 350°F / gas mark 4 for 40–45 minutes or until the juices run clear. Drain off the juice into another bowl as this is then used for the peppercorn sauce.

For the sauce:

1 Tbsp crushed peppercorns
½ onion, finely chopped
1 tsp vegetable oil (plus juice from the meat loaf)
150ml / 5 fl. oz double cream
½ stock cube (beef)
good splash of red wine
tomato purée

In another pan place finely chopped onions, oil and crushed peppercorns and sauté for a few minutes. Add the juices from the loaf and the red wine. Simmer for a few minutes then add a stock cube and thicken with tomato purée. Finally, add the double cream.

Leek and spinach potato cakes   serves 6

750g / 1½ lb potatoes
2 Tbsp vegetable oil
150g / 5 oz mushrooms
2 medium-sized leeks
250g / 9 oz spinach
1 tsp nutmeg
150g / 5 oz Lancashire cheese (grated)
1 egg (medium sized)
100g / 4 oz breadcrumbs
salt and pepper

Chop the potatoes and boil them until just tender. Mash the potatoes until fluffy. Heat the oil then sauté the chopped mushrooms and leeks until just tender. Place them on kitchen paper to absorb some of the oil. Then place the spinach in the pan and sauté for a couple of minutes; again, place on kitchen paper.

When the potato is cool add the nutmeg and mix well. Add the spinach, mushrooms and leeks to the potato mixture. Add the grated cheese. Mix well. Add salt and pepper to taste.

Divide into 6 equal portions and shape into potato cakes. Beat the egg in a bowl then roll the potato cakes in both the egg and the breadcrumbs.

Bake in the oven at 170°C / 350°F / gas mark 3 for 25 minutes and serve immediately.

Spinach and nut roast   serves 6

1 Tbsp vegetable oil
1 onion (chopped)
200g / 8 oz chopped mixed nuts
1 tsp dried basil
2 tsp yeast extract
300ml / 12 fl. oz vegetable stock
handful of breadcrumbs
100g / 4 oz spinach
1 tsp nutmeg
filo pastry (12 sheets)
salt and pepper

Heat the oil in a pan and add the chopped onions. Sauté for 2 minutes then add the nuts and basil and continue to cook for a further minute. Stir in the yeast extract then add the vegetable stock. Let it simmer for a couple of minutes then gradually add the breadcrumbs to bind all the ingredients together.

In a separate pan, sauté the spinach with a little salt and nutmeg. Immediately the spinach has wilted, remove from the pan. Chop the spinach mixture and mix in with the nut mixture. Check seasoning to taste and allow to cool.

Cut the filo pastry into even squares (approx 12cm / 5in square). Grease one square, then place another on top of it and grease that one. Place a portion of the mixture in the middle of the pastry square and then fold the square to make a neat parcel. Repeat 6 times.

Place greaseproof paper on the oven tray and place the parcels on top. Bake in the oven at 170°C / 325°F / gas mark 3 for 10 minutes until golden brown. Serve immediately.

Frozen lemon cream   serves 4–6

410ml / 14 fl. oz evaporated milk
150g / 6 oz icing sugar
juice and rind of ½ a lemon
150g / 6 oz digestive biscuits, crushed
50g / 2 oz butter

Ensure the tin of evaporated milk has been in the freezer for around 3 to 4 hours before you begin this recipe, so that it is on its way to being frozen. Once this has been done it should be of a thick consistency.

Place it in a mixing bowl and using an electric whisk slowly add the icing sugar.

Whisk until the mix doubles in size then slowly stir in the lemon rind and juice.

Melt the butter and add it to the digestive biscuits, mixing till all the butter is absorbed by the biscuits.

Grease a 10-inch flan ring and place the digestive biscuit mix in it, pressing down so that it is firm.

Using a spatula scoop out the lemon cream mix and place on the biscuit base. Smooth out and place in freezer. Serve straight from the freezer as this dessert melts quite quickly.

Note: you could also experiment with other fruits, e.g. orange or lime.

And the loaf is rising

Bread recipes

Note: each recipe makes 2 loaves. Bread tins should not be used.

Celeriac and Lancashire cheese bread

300g / 12 oz celeriac (grated)
200g / 8 oz crumbled Lancashire cheese
300g / 12 oz self-raising flour
8 spring onions (finely chopped)
good pinch of cayenne pepper
2 tsp salt
2 large eggs
4 Tbsp milk
2 tsp English mustard, powder or wet (optional)

Mix all dry ingredients together and then add all the wet ingredients, ensuring both your hands and the work surface have flour on them. Work into 2 loaves of suitable size, place on a greased tray and bake at 190°C / 375°F / gas mark 5 for 40–45 minutes.

Parsnip bread

1kg / 2 lb mashed parsnips
50g / 2 oz butter
1kg / 2 lb granary flour
3 tsp dried yeast
2 tsp salt
50g / 2 oz lard
450ml / 15 fl. oz water (tepid) or milk

Mix yeast and water and leave in a warm place for 5–10 minutes till a foam rises. In a separate bowl mix together the flour, mashed parsnips, salt, butter and lard. Gradually pour in yeast solution. Form into a dough and leave in a warm place to prove. When it has risen a little, knead the dough, place on a greased tray and leave to rise again for approx. 40 minutes. Bake at 200°C / 400°F / gas mark 6 for 30 minutes.

Sage and onion bread

2 large onions, finely chopped
50g / 2 oz butter
50g / 2 oz lard
500g / 1 lb strong white flour
500g / 1 lb strong wholemeal flour
3 tsp dried yeast
520ml / 1 pt water (tepid) or milk
2 tsp salt
pepper to season
2 tsp dried sage

Follow the same method as for the bread above.
Bake at 230°C / 450°F / gas mark 8 for 15 minutes then reduce to 200°C / 400°F / gas mark 6 for 15 minutes.

Autumn soups

Parsnip and apple   serves 4–6

3 parsnips
1 cooking apple
1 onion
50g / 2 oz butter
780ml / 1½ pt vegetable stock
1 tsp mixed herbs
270ml / ½ pt milk
salt
pepper

Peel and chop the parsnips and onion. Chop the apple in half, deseed and chop roughly.

In a pan add the butter and when it has melted add the onion and mixed herbs. Sauté till the onion is transparent then add the parsnips and apple.

Stir and leave to infuse for about 5 minutes then add the vegetable stock and bring to the boil. Once boiling reduce the heat and allow to simmer till the parsnips become soft.

Turn off the heat and let it cool down. Then blend and add milk.

Turn the heat back on and slowly simmer the soup. Add seasoning as required and serve.

Roasted red pepper and fennel   serves 4–6

2 red peppers
1 fennel bulb
½ onion
1l / 2 pt vegetable stock
50ml / 2 fl. oz orange juice
1 tsp lime zest plus ½ of the juice
1 tsp lemon zest plus ½ of the juice
½ red chilli
2 spring onions
pinch of salt and pepper
1 tsp cumin (ground)
½ tsp coriander (ground)
small bunch of coriander (fresh)
1 tsp tomato purée
1 tsp sugar
2 cloves of garlic
25g / 1 oz ginger (fresh)
1 Tbsp vegetable oil

Chop fennel into quarters and place on a tray with a little oil. Roast till it softens. Meanwhile roast the red peppers over an open flame till they blister. Then peel off the burnt skin, quarter and deseed.

Dice onion, chilli (deseeded and chopped), spring onions and garlic. Grate lemon and lime zest.

Once the fennel is soft pour any excess oil into a pan and heat. Add onion, ginger, garlic and chilli. Sauté for a few minutes.

Add ground cumin and coriander. Cook for a few minutes and add the fennel and red peppers. Cook a little longer. Add orange juice and then the vegetable stock and tomato purée. Bring to the boil then turn down the heat before adding the zest of lemon and lime. Simmer for 20–30 minutes.

Take off the heat and allow to cool a little, then add the coriander. Blend in a food processor for a minute or two until you end up with a smooth, orange soup. Add lime juice, sugar and season with salt and pepper to taste.

Finally add spring onions and serve.

Broccoli and Stilton   serves 4–6

2 small heads of broccoli
1 onion, chopped
2 carrots, grated
2 Tbsp vegetable oil
780ml / 1½ pt vegetable stock
salt
pepper
½ tsp mixed herbs
25g / 1 oz Stilton cheese
40ml / 1½ fl. oz double cream

Chop the broccoli into florets, saving the broccoli stems.

Make up the vegetable stock in a small pan and add the broccoli stems. (This will give the soup extra flavour.)

In another pan heat up the oil and add the chopped onion. Sauté for 2 minutes then add the broccoli florets, grated carrots and mixed herbs. Sauté for a further 5–10 minutes.

Remove the broccoli stems from the stock and carefully pour the stock on to the vegetables. Bring to the boil. Once boiling, turn down the heat and simmer until the broccoli is soft.

Turn off the heat and allow the soup to cool before blending it to a smooth consistency.

Crumble in the Stilton cheese and add cream and seasoning according to taste.

Winter soups

Crème du Barry

1 potato
1 onion
1 cauliflower
25g / 1 oz butter
50g / 2 oz strong Cheddar cheese (grated)
520ml / 1 pt vegetable stock
520ml / 1 pt milk
2 Tbsp chopped parsley
ground nutmeg to taste
seasoning to taste

Peel and chop the onion and potato. Break the cauliflower into florets.

Melt butter in a large saucepan and sauté the onion until transparent. Add all ingredients except the milk and cheese and bring to the boil. Reduce the heat, cover and simmer for 25 minutes.

Remove from the heat and add milk. When cool, blend in a liquidizer then reheat gently. Add grated cheese just before serving.

Armenian   serves 4–6

50g / 2 oz red lentils
50g / 2 oz dried apricots
1 large potato
1l / 2 pt vegetable stock
juice of ½ lemon
1 tsp ground cumin
2 Tbsp chopped parsley
seasoning to taste

Peel and roughly chop the potato then place all the ingredients in a large pan. Bring to the boil, cover and allow to simmer for 30 minutes.

Cool, then blend in a liquidizer. Reheat before serving.

Tomato and lentil   serves 4–6

1 onion, peeled and roughly chopped
50g / 2 oz red lentils
½ tsp dried basil
1 tsp tomato purée
400g / 1 lb tomatoes (tinned)
1 tsp yeast extract
780ml / 1½ pt vegetable stock

This soup is quick and simple for those who are always in a rush!

Heat the oil in a pan and then add the chopped onions and dried basil. Cook until the onions are transparent, then add the tomatoes and allow to simmer for approximately 5 minutes.

Add the red lentils and continue to simmer for approximately 5 minutes.

Stir in the yeast extract and add the vegetable stock. Bring to the boil and then turn down the heat and let it simmer for approximately 20 minutes, stirring regularly so that the lentils do not stick on the bottom of the pan.

Add more stock to thin the soup according to taste.

Add tomato purée. Season to taste.